Looking after MINI

Looking after MINI

HOW TO EXTEND THE LIFE OF A 20TH CENTURY ICON

1959-2000

TED CONNOLLY

MRP PUBLISHING LTD
PO Box 1318, Croydon CR9 5YP, England

First published 2004

Copyright © Ted Connolly 2004

All rights reserved. No part of this publication may be reproduced, stored in a retrieval system, or transmitted, in any form or by any means, electronic, mechanical, photocopying, recording or otherwise, without the prior permission in writing of the publishers

British Library Cataloguing in Publication Data
A catalogue record for this book is available from the British Library

ISBN 1-899870-68-7

Typesetting by Jack Andrews Design, Westerham, Kent
Printed and bound in Great Britain by The Amadeus Press, Cleckheaton, West Yorkshire

Contents

CHAPTER 1
    Choosing a Mini   9
    What to buy and where: the right Mini at the right price

CHAPTER 2
    Equipping your workshop   17
    Tools, their use and your working environment

CHAPTER 3
    The engine   21
    Overhauling with care, cleanliness and patience

CHAPTER 4
    Gearbox, clutch and transmission   37
    Inspection, overhaul and jobs for the specialists

CHAPTER 5
    The cooling system   42
    Diagnosing the fault can be more difficult than finding the cure

CHAPTER 6
    The electrical system   49
    Starter, charging and ignition systems and equipment

CHAPTER 7
> **Brakes, suspension and steering** 70
> Inspection, adjustment and replacement

CHAPTER 8
> **The fuel system** 88
> Fault-finding and carburettor tuning

CHAPTER 9
> **The bodywork** 94
> Panel repairs, replacement and paint spraying

CHAPTER 10
> **The interior** 106
> Time to repair or time to replace

CHAPTER 11
> **Upgrading your Mini** 108
> Sensible modifications for reliability, performance improvement and sheer driving pleasure

> **Mini facts and Mini-lore** 119
> Some things you may or may not have known

Preface

The Mini ranks as one of the most successful cars in the world – ever. It has been raced, rallied, filmed for the silver screen, customized, vaunted as an icon of the Sixties and – at the other end of the spectrum – served as an everyday hack for millions.

The motoring public's love affair with the Mini cannot be dispensed with simply by using an all-embracing phrase. Its charms are manifold. Mechanical simplicity – relatively speaking – is a major factor. It will never ask for much more than a reasonably good toolkit and pure tender, loving care. Economy and manoeuvrability are also key factors. But perhaps its greatest attraction is its sheer, chic character. Nothing can stifle its presence.

If driving a Mini can bring immeasurable pleasure then so, too, can the hands-on approach. That is, everything from routine maintenance to a complete restoration. The satisfaction can be immense. I've owned more than a dozen Minis – including a rorty Cooper S – and over the years made plenty of mistakes and unashamedly admit to turning out some forgettable work. But surely, mistakes are there to teach you; a person who makes no mistakes makes nothing.

Fortunately, dogged pride is not one of my considerable list of failings, and I have never been frightened to ask. And ask. And ask. And then put the many pieces of advice into practice. The beauty of gathering knowledge is that you can't erase it, only add to it. And that, of course, is the purpose of this book.

There is no doubt that many of you will already be well-equipped – in the workshop and ability senses. There is also no doubt that at least an equal number will be total novices, eager to embark on a first project. To slightly distort a common phrase – and, possibly, sound a little sexist – no book can be all things to all men. But whatever your level of competence, I promise that you will gather a great deal of useful information.

I not only advise, but indeed politely insist, that the first piece of armoury in your toolkit must be a workshop manual because that is precisely what this book is not. It was never intended to be some form of engineer's bible. Rather, it complements such rigid publications and examines aspects of maintenance and restoration which – although covered in part in other publications – have rarely been presented in detail and then put together as one package between two covers. It's aimed equally at the enthusiast with limited funds and knowledge and the restorer for whom expense is a secondary consideration.

Some of the advice will doubtless fly in the face of purists who insist that everything, but everything, must be carried out according to tradition. I make absolutely no apology for that. But the approach and methods you will read about have been tried and tested, they work well and are based on the practices and experience of many, many builders, from enthusiastic amateurs to respected professionals.

Naturally, not every job will be within your scope – such as the need for precision engineering – and if that's the case then I'll say so and make no bones about it. But by and large, there isn't much you can't tackle with patience and the right tools, and this book will take you from start to finish – from choosing a Mini, through maintaining it and, if you're seriously committed, tackling a complete restoration.

There is also a section on sensible modifications and performance tuning – modifications which will update your Mini, improve its efficiency and reliability and allow you to firmly stamp your own personality on it without compromising its charisma.

Fortunately, the Mini is so popular that there is no shortage of specialist companies and clubs. In short, the components and expertise abound.

I seriously recommend that you read and digest this book in its entirety rather than perusing sections piecemeal. The reason is that many of the subjects covered are interlinked and, to put it in simple terms, you need to see the big picture.

Above all, whatever your aims and reasons are for living with a Mini, never lose sight of what ownership is all about. Pure enjoyment.

Ted Connolly

CHAPTER 1

Choosing a Mini

What to buy and where:
the right Mini at the right price

CONSIDERING that more than five million Minis have been manufactured – albeit that a fair proportion have long since left the road through damage, rust or just pure age – it goes almost without saying that you're spoilt for choice. In fact, you are limited only by budget and personal preference.

Despite the Mini's massive lifespan, the concept has remained the same, and in essence very little has changed. The same, ever-faithful A-Series engine has been used throughout and, for the most part, the body has survived virtually unaltered.

The engine sizes fall into three categories – 850, 1000 and 1275 (apart from the now-rare versions such as the 1071cc Cooper S) – and body styles are saloon, Countryman, Estate, Clubman, Minivan and Mini Pick-up.

It has to be said that if you want a reasonable turn of performance and are considering tuning the engine, the 850 versions are non-starters. They simply don't have the cubic capacity to form the basis of a potent car. However, should you happen upon an 850 in exceptional condition, fitting a larger engine is relatively simple, thanks to the visionary design which was laid down from the start.

As for price, that's an almost open-ended question. You can pick up a well-worn example for little more than a couple of hundred pounds.

At the other end of the scale, an immaculate 1275 Cooper S could well fetch three to four thousand pounds, reflecting the esteem in which they are held.

Whatever the case, the same fundamental checks should be made and any differences for particular models will be pointed out. As with almost any secondhand car, the prime consideration is corrosion. Fortunately, the Mini is not known as a rot-box. However, rust can attack structural areas and that's your starting point. Examine the floorpan carefully, both from the underside and by lifting the carpets. It's delightfully simple to hide rust with metal plates blind-riveted (rather than welded) in place so, from above, you should expect to find smooth, clean metal, preferably with the paintwork still intact. Examine the seat fixings and beware if one or more of the bolts has pulled through.

The door sills are potential victims of corrosion so carefully check their condition from the inside and then the underside. The sills are load-bearing and, thus, an MoT failure point.

Replacement is not expensive, although it's a job for a competent welder.

Fresh underbody sealant on the underside should raise questions. Ask the seller why it is there. If a section has been repaired professionally and the car has a current MoT certificate from a reputable garage then you can be reasonably sure

Where it all began. It's 1959 and the Mini name is yet to catch on – this is one of the earliest cars, badged as the Austin Seven.

that the metal is now sound. The front subframe carries the engine and gearbox and, obviously, is vital for safety. Luckily, they rarely rot, mainly because over the years they get covered with a film of oil from the engine. In fact, I have never come across a corroded one.

However, the story is different at the rear where – subjected to water and salt from the roads – the subframe can collapse after several years. An inspection is crude and mucky, but it must be done. Poke every section of the subframe with a stout screwdriver, and if any of the metal gives way then you know that replacement is imminent. Making a bodge repair with body filler and then copious amounts of underbody sealant is an afternoon's work and can be difficult to detect – even some MoT testers have been fooled – so, as a secondary precaution, check the metal with a magnet.

Replacing a rear subframe is by no means technically difficult and relatively inexpensive for a competent DIY mechanic. But it is an exceedingly time-consuming and dirty job and one which I would rather avoid unless the car being viewed had other attributes which made it particularly desirable, such as exceptional paintwork, a totally immaculate interior or uncommonly low mileage.

A dirty engine is not necessarily a bad engine. However, first impressions when lifting the bonnet will give you a good idea of how much care – or otherwise – has been lavished on the car.

Lift the carpets to inspect the floor. A repair such as this is acceptable provided the welding has been carried out properly. However, if it has been necessary to weld in new metal this could be an indication of the condition of the rest of the floor, so carry out a very careful check.

Other potential corrosion spots are the bottoms of the doors, inside the boot (especially where the battery sits), the front wings where they meet the windscreen scuttle and the A-panels, which sit between the front wings and the door pillars.

On the Countryman, water can get trapped between the wood sections and the bodywork and lead to corrosion. The wood itself – like all timber – will gradually deteriorate with time. If it's started to rot right through then that is an expensive repair. Replacements are available, but they are costly. However, if the wood is in basically sound condition it will respond well to sanding and varnishing.

Early Minis had sliding windows. Not the most convenient of ideas, but it meant that generous door pockets could be used because there was no window-winder mechanism to take up space. Moisture can gather in and around the felt sliders and start the rot. I discovered that to my cost when slamming the door of a supposedly superb Cooper S and was rewarded with the complete assembly falling into the car.

Now for that A-Series engine, which must rank as one of the most proven and trustworthy units to have graced a British car. The fact that, quite apart from the Mini, the same basic engine has powered the Morris Minor, BMC 1100 and 1300, Sprite, Midget and Metro in various guises speaks volumes for its inherent robustness and dependability.

By today's standards, it is an unashamedly old-fashioned unit, with carburettors, OHV as opposed to overhead camshaft and non-crossflow head. But old-fashioned means uncomplicated in this case, and that equates to few faults and ease of maintenance. In fact, the only real weak point of this engine is the timing chain. Listen for a rattly, flailing sound from the area around the crankshaft pulley, by the radiator. If it is pronounced you know the chain will need replacing; a fiddly but simple enough procedure. Take comfort from the fact that the timing chain will complain for many miles before failing, although it is a job which should not be postponed indefinitely.

If you are looking at a Cooper, pay extra attention to the chain because it is of the duplex variety on these models and by now quite expensive.

If there are any oil leaks, it's an almost certain bet that they will be from either the rocker cover or the tappet covers at the back of the engine. A cure is easily effected. Expect a certain amount of noise from the tappets. In fact, it's better to have a tappety engine than one on which the valve gear is completely silent, because that would suggest that the clearances have been over-tightened, which would quickly burn out the valves.

It's important to test drive any secondhand car for several miles because faults not apparent in a roadside check could well manifest themselves when the car has been thoroughly warmed-up.

That is especially the case with the Mini's cooling system. You could hardly describe the Mini as a potential kettle, but because the radiator is mounted sideways and not in the direct flow of air, there is a tendency for the system to boil over if it has not been well maintained. Obvious signs of overheating are a temperature gauge which passes beyond the halfway mark and a heater which blows cold air. A further check can be made when the test drive has finished. Listen for hissing sounds from the radiator cap and look for leaks from hoses, caused by excessive pressure. On no account attempt to remove the radiator cap until the engine has cooled because there is a risk of being showered by scalding coolant.

During the test drive, floor the throttle with the car in top gear to check for clutch slip. This will also give you a rough guide to the condition of the bottom end. If the big-ends are suspect they will knock with the engine under heavy load. But don't confuse this with pre-ignition (or pinking) from the top of the engine. This is usually caused by over-advanced ignition or the wrong grade of fuel.

Another check on the bearings is made by observing the oil pressure gauge (when fitted). When the engine is hot, the gauge should register at least 25psi at tickover and immediately flick round to 50–75psi when the engine is revved.

The gears should change smoothly, but with the so-called 'magic wand' gearstick on early models, you must accept that the change is somewhat agricultural. If the car slips out of gear (especially first) the chances are that the layshaft has worn or one or more of the detent springs is worn. This will entail a gearbox overhaul. With the Cooper variants, this is particularly significant because a gearbox rebuild is considerably more expensive than on standard models.

At the end of the test run, get the seller to rev the engine reasonably hard and watch the exhaust. Black smoke indicates an over-rich mixture, which is easily adjusted. However, clouds of blue smoke mean that either the rings and bores are worn or the valve guides need replacing. The chances are that you are looking at a rebore and new pistons.

A decade or so ago it would have been unreasonable to expect a Mini engine to cover more than, say, 90,000 miles without the need for a complete overhaul. However, with modern oils, the A-Series engine will happily cover considerably more than 100,000 miles. The key, of course, is regular oil and filter changes, and while a seller will not always be honest about the car's history, checking the dipstick will tell you a good deal about the way it has been treated. If the oil is black and thin it is a fair bet that it has not been changed for a while, which is an indicator of how much or little care has been dispensed.

Testing the brakes and steering is simple. The car should pull up sharply and in a straight line – find a suitably quiet stretch of road to check this – and there should be no steering bias. If the car pulls to one side under braking it is probably down to poor adjustment (front drums) or worn pads (discs).

A permanent steering bias signifies either maladjusted tracking or a worn rack. With the former you will almost certainly find that the front tyres have scrubbed on their edges, leading to uneven tread wear. Turn the wheel to full-lock one way and then opposite-lock while you drive. This will tell you much about the condition of the constant-velocity joints. Worn or soon-to-fail CVs will protest with a pronounced cracking sound when put to the test under full-lock.

The Mini's most widely fitted suspension

Don't be put off by minor pitting on chrome, which can be dealt with using wire wool and a good-quality polish.

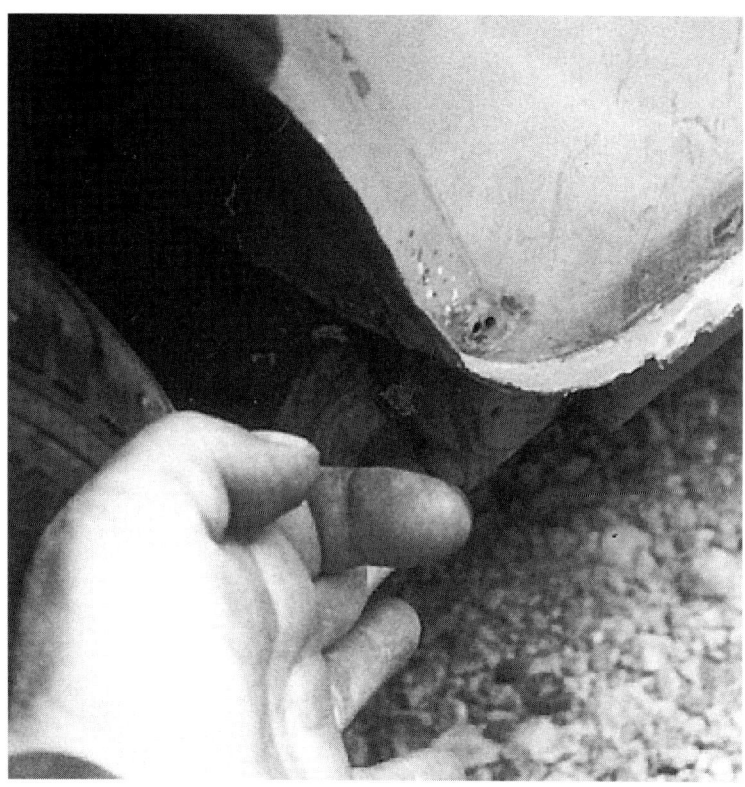

This area of the bodywork is prone to rusting. Minor scabs can be dealt with easily, but a hole in the metal means a welding job.

system is crude in the extreme – rubber cones and shock absorbers – but it is also amazingly effective. If the car sits evenly on the road and none of the tyres catches the bodywork under reasonably hard cornering then all should be well.

The alternative Hydrolastic suspension system is now relatively rare. Should you view a Mini with this set-up then, once again, make sure that it sits evenly on the road and that none of the corners sags. Press down on each corner and the other end should lift noticeably, which means that the displacer units are functioning correctly. If replacement is considered necessary bear in mind that specialist equipment is needed to de-pressurize and re-pressurize the system. The equipment and expertise is still available in the trade although relatively few garages are capable of carrying out the work these days.

Now it is a case of making a series of general checks on the lights, indicators, washers and wipers, horn, both door locks plus the lock on the boot, and the exhaust. Faults in any of these areas are by no means major causes for concern, but you need to know what extra expense you will be facing, and you may be able to use minor problems as a lever to bring down the price.

Documentation, of course, is important and, at the very least, check that the details on the registration document make sense. For example, if the registered keeper has a different address to the seller then ask why. It could be that the seller is a dealer and acting quite legitimately. However, those in the trade will always ask significantly higher prices than private sellers.

Check the mileage on the MoT certificate and compare it with the reading on the odometer. That way you have at least some sort of assurance that the odometer reading is reasonably accurate. You can also gauge how many miles the car has covered over the past year. If it's huge it is a pretty certain bet that the Mini has been used as a workhorse and could have been given a hard time.

One important point regarding the MoT certificate: this is absolutely no guarantee that the car is in a roadworthy condition. It means quite

A Mini cabriolet is a tempting option, but if you choose the soft-top route make sure that it is either a genuine factory model or that the conversion has been carried out professionally; ask to see the paperwork. The bodyshell needs to be strengthened to compensate for the lack of a roof, hence this is not a job for an amateur.

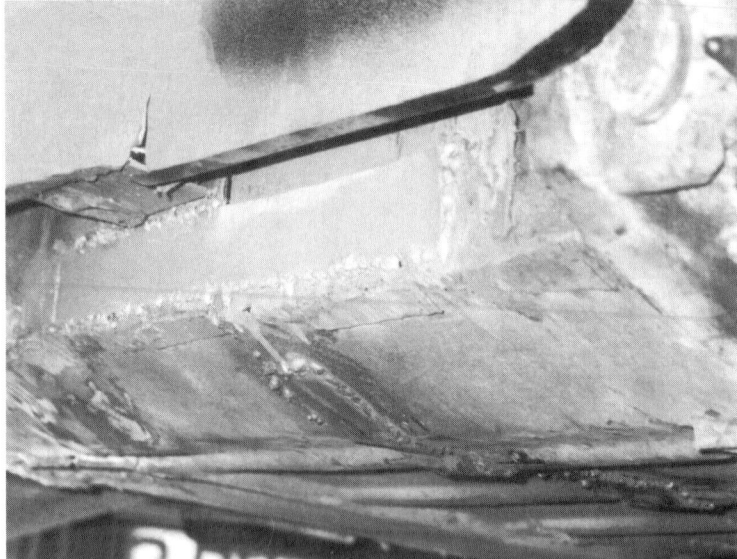

It's a dirty job, but it has to be done. Inspect as much of the underside as you can, looking for corrosion and attempts to hide it with underbody sealant.

Here's a favourite rust spot – the bottom of a door. Although scabs are acceptable and treatable, major rust means a new door skin will be required.

The Mini can rot almost anywhere, as demonstrated here. This Mini has been stripped for restoration and repairs to the rear seat support. A competent welder will be capable of patching the damaged metal.

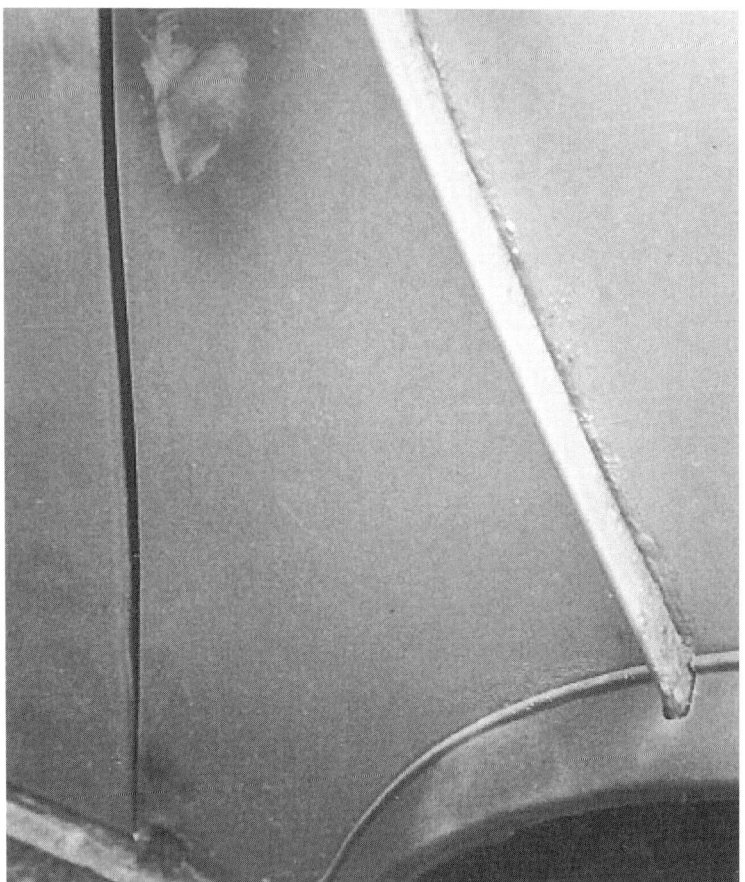

The A-panels are a known rust point on a Mini. In this instance, replacement will soon be required.

simply that it was fit for the road when tested, nothing more and nothing less. So treat a valid MoT as a welcome bonus, but not a cast-iron assurance that the Mini is completely sound.

Perhaps one of the best checks you can make on any secondhand car is to pretend it is your own vehicle, then ask yourself this question: 'If it were mine, would it be in this sort of condition bearing in mind its age and mileage?' If the answer is 'Yes', the documentation checks out, the drive is pleasant and there are no undue rattles or knocks from the engine and gearbox, then the chances are that this Mini is worth buying.

The Mini is renowned for developing corrosion at the tops of the wings where they meet the windscreen scuttle. In this instance, a new wing and scuttle will almost certainly be needed within a year.

This level of corrosion on the windscreen pillars can be dealt with by using a rust converter. However, a hole is tricky to deal with, so if in doubt, look elsewhere for your purchase.

On earlier Minis with sliding windows, pay particular attention to the sliders, which can rot right through. Although this area is not such a problem on later versions with wind-up windows, corrosion can form beneath the chrome strip.

CHAPTER 2

Equipping your workshop

Tools, their use and your working environment

ACCORDING to the old saying, a bad workman always blames his tools. But it's an even poorer workman who has no tools to blame. Having the right equipment will not only make life immeasurably easier, it will also make working on your Mini significantly more pleasurable.

I would hardly insult you by listing in great detail what you need as basics. Suffice to say your toolkit should include a set of open-ended and ring spanners, a half-inch drive socket set (preferably backed up with a three-eighths drive set for the finer jobs), a selection of screwdrivers, pliers and hammers, a set of feeler gauges, stroboscopic timing light, valve spring compressor, a decent trolley jack and either axle stands or wheel ramps. On a point of safety, remember that a jack raises a car and axle stands or wheel ramps support it. Never, ever get underneath a car held purely by a jack. That is asking for disaster.

The Mini requires relatively few special tools. The one which will undoubtedly be used the most is a ball-joint splitter, and there are two types. One is a wedge-section fork which is hammered on to a tapered shaft to separate it. The other uses a bolt and jaws. This type is probably twice as dear as the wedge-shaped splitter, but it is very progressive and rarely causes damage to the gaiter.

The SU carburettor is adjusted by turning the jet-height nut at the base of the body and a special spanner is available for this. However, it's not vital to have one of these because a conventional spanner will do the job, but the pukka tool is small and thin and, thus, allows easy access.

Changing the clutch on a Mini means separating the flywheel from the end of the crankshaft and you will need the puller for this job, and if you tackle the rubber-cone suspension you will need a compressor. It is little more than a bolt which screws into the centre of the cone and facilitates its removal. Generally speaking, that's it as far as tools peculiar to the Mini are concerned.

Few things get cheaper as time progresses, but with many tools, prices have dropped noticeably, thanks to modern production methods, also to the major retailers who deal in large quantities which can be bought from suppliers at competitive prices. So the type of equipment which was once firmly the domain of the professional is now easily within the budget of the DIY mechanic.

Now let's look at tools which, although they could hardly be regarded as essential, are an absolute boon when working on cars. To me, a compressor ranks high on the chart of must-haves – possibly number one. The most obvious use for a compressor, of course, is paint-spraying. But it will also power a huge variety of tools, such as sanders, grinders, air-chisels and pneumatic

This is a ball-joint splitter. It works progressively by gradually tightening the bolt. Although more expensive, this type is preferable to the wedge type, which has to be used with a hammer.

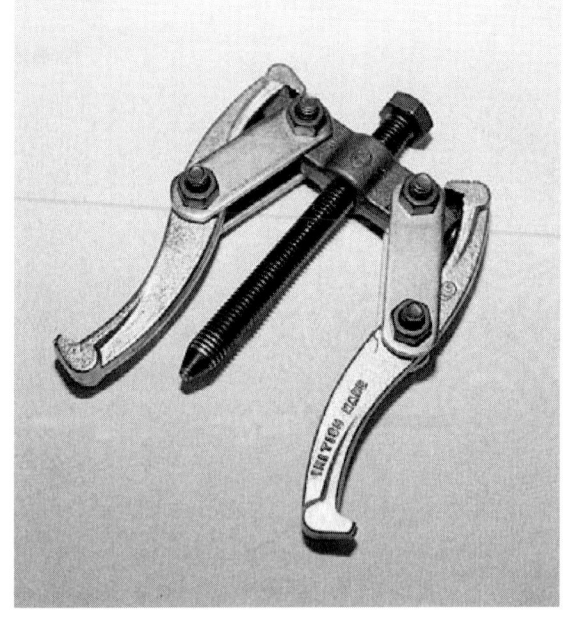

A universal puller is an incredibly handy piece of equipment, for example when removing a front hub. Buy one with reversible legs, as pictured, which will grip on either internal or external surfaces.

spanners and, with a nozzle, will provide an excellent means of cleaning loose dirt and swarf from components.

You could be tempted to buy a cheap compressor – and some are remarkably inexpensive – but avoid anything with a collector tank of less than 50 litres, otherwise you are likely to run out of puff when, for example, spraying large areas. A decent compressor will give years of service, provided the oil and intake filter are changed regularly and the collector tank drained at intervals specified by the manufacturer. Before I bought mine, it seemed like a luxury I could do without. Now, about a decade later and with the same piece of equipment, it's something I can't ever imagine not having.

You might, perhaps, wonder why it is worth bothering with air tools when you can buy their electrical equivalents. Well, there are several reasons. For a start, they are usually lighter and more compact. There are very few moving parts and, therefore, they should last longer. From the safety point of view, if you're working in damp conditions there is absolutely no chance of suffering an electric shock. And they are convenient. If you are alternating between two or more tools, all you need do is have them to hand and attach each to the airline at will.

If a compressor is a great friend in the workshop then so, too, is a welder. Welding falls into three basic categories – gas, arc and MIG. Quite frankly, I never have and never would bother with gas-welding. It is a skilled process and the equipment is both bulky and relatively expensive. Arc-welding (also known as stick-welding) is another method which has never appealed to me. It does provide an immensely strong joint, but it can also be brutal on panels such as wings and doors and will almost invariably leave untidy slag.

By far the best method, in my opinion, is MIG – Metal Inert Gas – welding. The welding wire is shielded by inert gas when it fuses with metal which (a) prevents slag and (b) keeps the surrounding areas cool and thus avoids distortion. With practice, it is clean, fast and efficient. MIG was succinctly explained to me by a professional thus: 'If you can solder, you can weld.' You've basically got just a few variables to play with – amperage, wire speed and the speed the nozzle is moved. If you read the instructions carefully and spend a day practising the chances are that you will be acceptably proficient.

Obviously, safety is of paramount importance and you should never weld near a fuel line or the petrol tank (remove it if necessary) nor use the equipment near cans of fuel, paint, etc. Always wear the correct goggles because the rays given off from the welding process can seriously damage your eyes. A MIG welder has a multiplicity of uses and will enable you to carry out repairs which would once have meant replacing components. Having said that, unless you are totally competent and confident, welding load-bearing structures should most definitely be left to the professionals.

A pressure washer could be regarded as a luxury and, to be fair, it isn't something you will use on a regular basis. But if you are seriously into mechanical work then put it on your shopping list as an imminent purchase. Most washers offer up to 1500psi of pressure (that's about 100 bar) and you will never need more than that. This piece of equipment is at its best when blasting clean really mucky components and you will find no better way of keeping your engine bay immaculate, which, as a bonus, makes mechanical work that much more pleasurable. It is also ideal

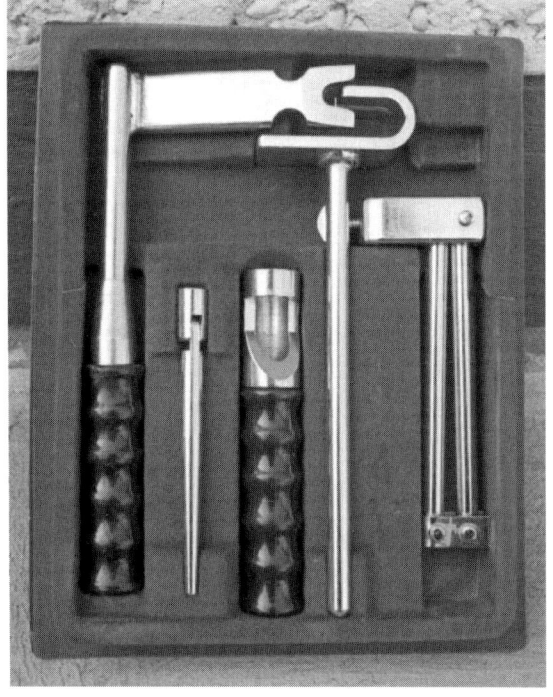

When dealing with brakes, you can usually get by using pliers, screwdrivers, etc. However, a pukka kit such as this provides everything you need for adjustment and replacement.

Mass production and the advent of DIY superstores has brought down the prices of tools dramatically, so consider among other items a pressure washer and paint-spraying equipment.

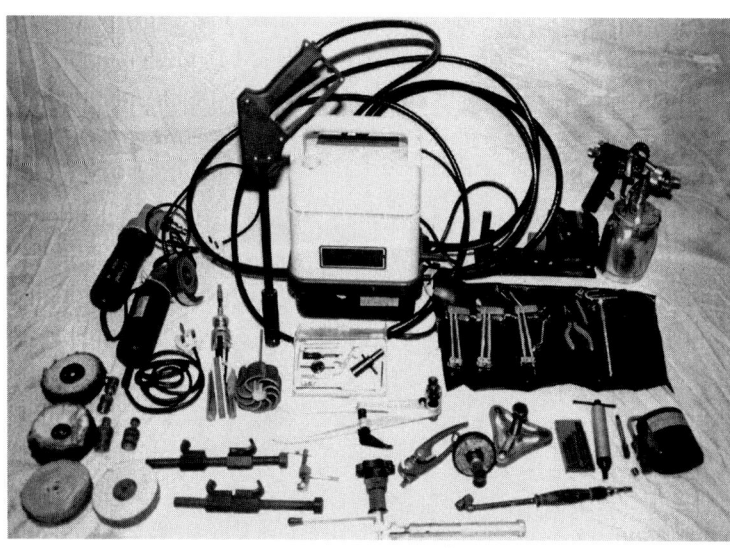

for keeping aluminium wheels in good order.

Two pieces of static – as opposed to portable – workshop equipment have won my unshakeable friendship over the years. They are a bench grinder and bench (or press) drill. The grinder has proved invaluable and, with polishing wheels fitted, many components have been transformed into objects of admiration (SU carbs being a good example). A bench drill affords you great accuracy – far greater than a hand drill – and

A compression check on your engine will tell you much about its condition. This type of gauge, which is at the cheaper end of the market, has to be held in place while the engine is turned. The more expensive gauges screw into the spark plug holes and therefore are more convenient to operate.

it's something which comes highly recommended.

You can add to your toolkit as money permits and necessity dictates and you will doubtless soon count items such as a cylinder compression gauge, circuit tester and torque wrench as an intrinsic part of your armoury. On a point of finance – and that must be close to many people's hearts – the most expensive parts of my toolkit are a compressor, two spray guns and various air tools, MIG welder, pressure washer, bench grinder, bench drill and stroboscopic timing light, which incorporates a rev-counter and dwell meter. When bought – something like a decade ago – the total bill came to more than £1000. Now, it would be possible to buy the equivalent kit for little over half that sum. Take inflation into account and you can appreciate just how much specialist tools have come down in price.

If you are blessed with the facility of a workshop then the rules are pretty simple – the ideal environment has light, warmth and dryness. With these three commodities you'll be fit to tackle virtually any job in comfort. Finally, and most importantly, make sure that the workshop and its contents are adequately covered by insurance.

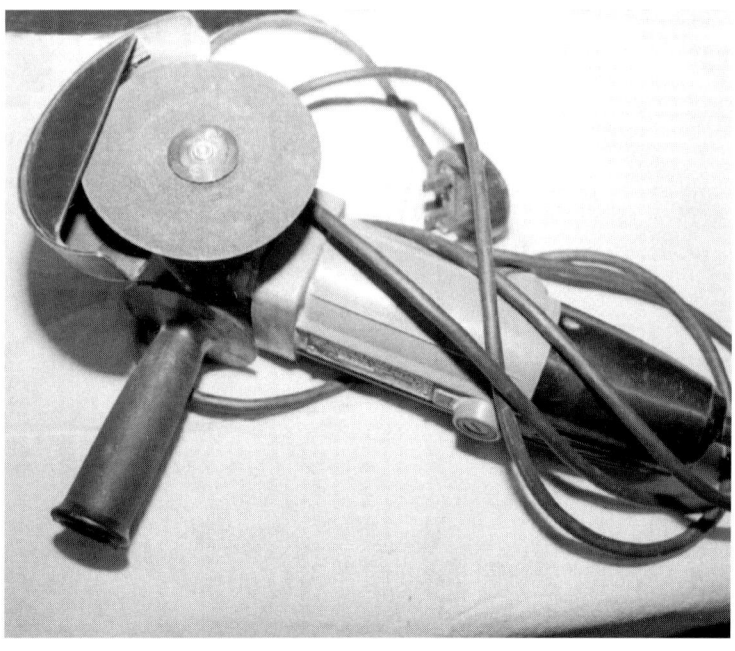

An angle-grinder is a versatile piece of equipment which will become much used, especially when dealing with bodywork.

CHAPTER 3

The engine

Overhauling with care, cleanliness and patience

COMPARED with modern engines, which are bristling with technology such as electronic control units, turbos, fuel injection and variable valve timing, the Mini's A-Series unit may be positively old-fashioned, but this is part of its charm. Its relative simplicity and fundamental reliability have been cornerstones of its use in a wide variety of other BMC-designed and produced cars in addition to the five million-plus Minis it has powered over more than four decades.

Versatile and friendly, the A-Series engine takes on something of a new perspective in the Mini because of its transverse layout, sitting over the gearbox and driving through the front wheels. Such a configuration, of course, means that although the maintenance and repair requirements are fundamentally similar to when the A-Series engine is installed in a conventional rear-wheel-drive car, some of the procedures are different because of more limited access. But practice brings familiarity and what at first might appear to be daunting tasks can become in time almost second nature.

With routine maintenance, the finest treat you can give the engine is regular oil and filter changes. Never exceed 6000 miles or six months (whichever comes the sooner) before carrying out this job. Follow this rule and you can literally double the life of an engine, and it is especially important to do so with the Mini installation in which the oil has to serve both the engine and the transmission. Even the experts disagree on which type of oil to use – mineral, semi-synthetic or synthetic – and there is no doubt that the synthetic types are superior. They are also significantly more expensive than the other two, and I have never found any argument to sway me from using a good quality mineral oil, changed along with the filter on a regular basis. If your engine lacks a magnetic sump plug, fit one because it will attract any swarf.

The other routine servicing task is to check and adjust the tappets. Many owners see this as merely a means of keeping the top end as quiet as possible, but although a sweet sounding engine is psychologically reassuring, keeping the valve clearances correctly adjusted is far more significant. It is a commonly held belief that a gap is necessary to allow for expansion, but if that were the case why adjust the tappets on some cars when the engine is hot and expansion has already taken place?

In fact there are two primary reasons for the clearance, the first being that when there is a gap, you know for certain that the valve is fully closed. With what is termed a working clearance, there can be no leakage on the compression stroke. The second reason concerns the camshaft profile. Every mass-production engine's components are

The A-Series engine is about as basic as they come, far removed from the complexity of modern power plants. But basic equates to ease of maintenance and repair – apart from the inevitable awkwardness of a few specific jobs.

made within certain tolerances, and although a camshaft is manufactured to a reasonably high level of accuracy, pure economics mean that there must be a degree of variation. In other words, the profile of every camshaft can vary, even if only to a small degree. Adjusting the valve clearance overcomes this and allows you to fine-tune the camshaft timing and duration of opening, in exactly the same way that you alter the ignition timing and dwell angle by setting the contact breaker gap. Admittedly, we are talking about small variations, but it can make a difference to your Mini's overall performance.

The tried-and-tested method of setting the tappets involves the rule-of-nine. As with any work on the engine, always disconnect the battery to avoid accidents. Remove the spark plugs and then the rocker cover. I've found that the easiest way to turn the engine is to put the car in fourth gear and rock it to and fro. Less energetic, but slightly more awkward, is to use a spanner on the crankshaft pulley bolt. When number one exhaust valve is open (rocker depressed), you should check the clearance on valve number eight (exhaust) at the other end of the engine. When valve number two (inlet) is open, check valve number seven (inlet) and so on. In other words, the valve open and the valve to be checked add up to nine. Just start on the outside and work your way in. Luckily, you have no need to worry about confusing inlets with exhausts because the settings are the same – 12 thou, and that reading is taken cold.

If the engine still sounds tappety when the clearances have been set, do not be tempted to close up the gaps. It almost certainly means that a step has worn in one or more of the rocker faces and they should be replaced. This is easily checked by removing the tappets, which are unbolted and come off as one unit. As a short-term measure, some owners grind the faces flat, but that's a false economy because you'll go through the case hardening and the rattle will return very shortly.

Setting the tappets with too small a clearance will at the very least rob the engine of compression. At worst, it will not allow the valves to stay seated on the head long enough to disperse heat and they will quickly burn out, particularly the exhausts.

Adjusting the valve clearances is a vital prelude to what is probably the most important health check you can make on the engine – a compression test. This will tell you much about its internal condition and help you decide what, if any, work is required. By far the best type of compression tester to use is one with a screw-in nozzle, which can be left in place while you briefly spin the engine on the starter (this test should be carried out with the throttle wide open

The rockers are easy to get at – simply remove the metal cover. Also, there is no worry about confusing inlets with exhausts because the tappet clearance is the same for both.

and the engine warm). Cheaper gauges have a tapered rubber nozzle which has to be physically held in place when the engine is turned, so without the help of a friend, the job is virtually impossible.

The key is to correctly interpret the readings. Ideally, an A-Series engine should show a compression of about 125psi per cylinder. However, if it is slightly lower – say 110psi – there is no cause for alarm provided the readings on each cylinder are within 10 per cent of each other. All that means is that the engine is worn, but it has worn evenly. However, if one of the cylinders is significantly down on compression you need to investigate further. Squirt clean engine oil down the spark plug hole of the offending cylinder and carry out another test. If the reading has gone up noticeably then the piston rings and/or bore are at fault.

Another check on the rings and bores is to spin the motor for several seconds to see if the reading gradually gets higher. If it does, you have almost certainly pinpointed the fault. If the engine is still performing satisfactorily and there is no excessive blue smoke in the exhaust, at this stage you can leave well enough alone but make a mental note that at some stage a rebore and new pistons will be necessary. However, if you can't pump up the reading and adding oil to the bores makes no difference, the problem is probably a leaking valve. Of course, a low compression reading could be caused by a leaking cylinder head gasket, but in that case you will almost certainly experience other symptoms such as loss of coolant or oil and a misfire.

The story doesn't quite end there because with the 1275cc versions you might get noticeably lower readings on the inner two cylinders because there is precious little metal between the combustion chambers (especially on the 1275 Cooper S) and subsequent head failure at this point is not uncommon.

At this juncture, I will assume that the compression readings are acceptable. The following is a routine which mechanics followed religiously for years, but is now virtually a forgotten practice because today's engines require little in the way of maintenance and adjustment. The routine is: plugs, points, timing, tappets, mixture. Observe this procedure and your engine should end up in perfect tune. The reason for the sequence is that the plugs, points, timing and tappets are all set scientifically – that is, with feeler gauges and a timing light – whereas setting the mixture is to an extent a matter of judgment and cannot be achieved until the other areas are in order.

Dealing with the plugs is totally routine and the only pieces of information worth noting are that the end-screw on each plug should be nipped up to avoid it becoming loose and causing a misfire, and to treat the threads to a copper-based grease to guard against seizure in the cylinder head. The ignition and fuel systems are covered elsewhere in the appropriate sections.

The A-Series engine usually remains oil-tight, mainly because it doesn't rev particularly quickly and is not subjected to excessive vibration, also because being completely cast-iron it doesn't have to contend with the different rates of expansion which apply with an engine with a cast-iron block and an aluminium cylinder head.

Two places where you may encounter leaks are from the rocker cover and the tappet covers, at the back behind the exhaust. Almost invariably, seepage is caused by over-tightening the retaining bolts and distorting the relatively thin metal. The cure is as basic as it is effective. In the case of the rocker cover, clean the component thoroughly and use an impact adhesive to stick a new gasket in place. You will then know there is absolutely no chance of oil getting past the joint and that the gasket will remain perfectly in position. Now use a

The feeler blade should be a firm, sliding fit between the rocker and valve. Imagine cutting butter with a knife and you get the idea.

gasket compound between the gasket and head. Unconventional, but it is guaranteed to work. And the same goes for the tappet cover.

Another potential leak point is from the timing chain cover oil seal. It sits in the cover behind the crankshaft pulley and spotting a leak is easy – get the engine warm, then let the car stand. Tell-tale drips of oil can be spotted from behind the pulley.

Fitting a new seal is not technically difficult, but it is a fiddly job. Once the crank pulley is off, the cover can be removed by undoing the series of bolts around its edge. It's the care in fitting the new seal and then the cover which pays dividends. The seal should be gently driven into place using a suitable drift (a large socket, for example) or piece of wood and mallet. It must go in square and without being damaged. The cover is then refitted and the bolts just nipped up so that the cover can move. Refit the crankshaft pulley and rotate the engine a few times. This will centralize the timing chain cover and, in theory, give you a perfectly oil-tight seal.

The most commonly known weak point of the A-Series engine is the timing chain, which can rattle annoyingly after a moderate mileage. It's an obvious enough fault to diagnose; just listen to the engine in the region of the radiator and the rattle will be self-evident. If you suspect the chain on your engine, an ideal time to change it is when you're tackling the oil seal.

The cog-wheels on the crank and camshaft have timing marks and they must be lined up when the chain is being fitted. You can make life simple by ensuring that the crank is not turned when the chain has been removed, and therefore remains in the correct position in relation to the camshaft.

Possibly one of the most annoying faults on the Mini is the tendency for the engine to rock on take-up of power and then to clunk alarmingly. This is caused by wear in the stabilizer bar bushes. The bar runs from engine to bulkhead, being bolted underneath the master cylinders. Change the rubbers and you will transform the feel of the car.

The screw-in type of compression tester is the most convenient because you can use it easily without having to call for assistance.

The most major job you are likely to carry out with the engine in-situ is to lift the head to replace the gasket, fit new valve springs or whatever. The first time I tackled this task, it took me more than a day. Now, having carried it out dozens of times, if the head is not off within about 90 minutes I start to feel that something is seriously wrong with my ability. It's a case of disconnecting all of the attachments – cables, hoses, fuel line and the exhaust – removing the rockers and pushrods (keep them in order, ideally by pushing them through a piece of cardboard and numbering it), and undoing the head nuts in the correct sequence.

The point of observing the loosening sequence on the head nuts is that the load is released progressively, which avoids distorting the head. Some owners prefer to remove the manifolds from the head, but I've always found it preferable to leave them attached and merely disconnect the exhaust system at the downpipe after taking off the clamp. It saves the annoyance of trying to get at the manifold nuts, and the carburettor serves as a useful handle when lifting the head.

If the head has never been off – which is quite likely – it may have fixed itself firmly to the block. Breaking the seal takes a few seconds – just turn the engine briefly on the starter and the compression will do the job for you. Since the head is cast-iron, distortion is rarely a problem, but it is definitely better to be cautious than rueful. Checking the condition of the head is vital because even a new gasket will not cure a leak if the surface is not true.

You check the head with a straight-edge – a steel rule is ideal. By holding the edge of the rule at various points on the face of the head, any distortion or damage will quickly become apparent. As mentioned earlier, there is not a great deal of metal between the middle two combustion chambers on the 1275 engine's head, so pay particular attention to this area. If there is any sign of cracking or burning of the metal then you will need an exchange head.

Genuine items for the Cooper S Mini are not that easy to come by, but that's no problem because there are many specialists around who can metal-spray and then skim the face. In fact, these firms are an absolute boon for reclaiming what you might at first consider to be an irreparable component.

Even if you reckon that the valves are in perfect condition, it would be foolish having come this far not to remove them for inspection, then lap them in. Bear in mind that the valve springs are under a fair bit of pressure, and unless a pukka compressor is used the collars can fly off at an alarming velocity. So don't try to make do with a home-made device. It's one of those tools for which there is no substitute. As an added precaution, never look down on a valve when you

The rocker cover gasket is prone to leaking. If it is damaged or noticeably compressed – as opposed to simply feeling springy to the touch – fit a new one, using impact adhesive to attach it to the cover *(see main text)*.

are removing the spring and collar just in case the compressor should slip. Always view it from the side.

Valve collets which have not been disturbed for a considerable time – maybe never – can be stubborn to dislodge. If you start compressing the spring and the collets go with it, give the fork of the compressor a sharp tap with a hammer and that will break the seal.

Assessing wear of the valve guides requires using your judgment. Wash the valve in a degreasant (petrol is ideal) and insert it three-quarters into the guide. Now waggle it side-to-side. There should be slight movement – about 1/16th of an inch at the valve head is permissible. If you are in doubt, but know that the engine was not smokey when being run, you can be sure that the valves and guides are in an acceptable condition.

If anything, I would prefer slightly worn guides because that allows oil to seep into the combustion chambers and provides upper cylinder lubricant. And with a small amount of wear, any oil in the chambers will soon clear itself.

I've come across all manner of gadgets for lapping in valves, but none is more effective than the stick and rubber sucker. Time-consuming, yes, but it always does the job accurately and with perfect control. You're aiming for an unbroken, clean ring of metal around each valve and its corresponding seat. Lap in using a coarse paste and follow up with a fine paste.

If a seat is deeply pitted or cracked it must be replaced. When each valve has been lapped in, you can make a detailed examination of the seat and any damage will be all the more apparent. Do not bother trying to remove damage to a seat by lapping in the valve even more because this will make it sit too deeply. This is known as pocketing and it will impede gas flow and, thus, affect performance.

Recutting or replacing seats is a job for a specialist and that goes for valve guides, too. If one or more of the seats needs replacing and the guides are worn, weigh up the cost of the repairs against that for a reconditioned head.

Carbon can be cleaned from the combustion chambers and valves using a blunt scraper. Be careful not to damage the valve contact areas. Cleanliness is the keyword with reassembly. Make absolutely sure that there is no grinding paste on the valve or the guides otherwise wear will be rapid.

You can measure the free length of the valve springs to discover whether they are still serviceable. But springs are so cheap and relatively inaccessible that I always fit a new set as a matter of course. With the valves back in place (and spark plugs screwed in), tip a small quantity of paraffin into each combustion chamber to check for leaks.

The surface of the block should also be checked with a straight-edge and you should make a careful examination for cracks. The Mini's block is not prone to damage unless the engine has seriously overheated, in which case you may detect hairline cracks. They are literally about as visible as a hair, but don't be fooled because with expansion they can widen enough to allow coolant to escape.

However, if the engine has always maintained its temperature prior to overhaul, almost certainly all will be well. Always fit a new head gasket (it will be marked 'top' and 'front') and never use a jointing compound.

On earlier engines there is a bypass hose which is connected between the block and head. Replace this regardless of condition because it is prone to failure, and replacing it is tricky without removing the head *(see the chapter on the cooling system)*.

The head studs should be tightened in the correct sequence to spread the load and you do this by starting at the centre and working outwards diagonally. The threads on the nuts and studs should be clean and dry because the torque settings are calculated on this basis, rather than with the aid of grease. As mentioned earlier, the pushrods should be replaced in the correct order because they will have worn in with their tappets and must continue to work in mechanical harmony.

One of the trickiest jobs when refitting the head is getting the exhaust downpipe to seal with the manifold. The latter is tapered and the exhaust downpipe belled out to suit. If you don't get the pair together properly the exhaust will leak which is (a) an MoT failure point and (b) a total irritation. Because access is limited, juggling the two together and then trying to fit the clamp is an incredible test of patience.

Instead, adopt this method: place a jack (a trolley jack is always preferable, but the scissor type will do) beneath the exhaust and raise it so that the pipe is sitting snugly against the manifold, but not so tightly that it cannot be moved. Now position it so that the belled section mates perfectly with the manifold. Raise the jack a small amount and the exhaust will stay in position and leave both of your hands free to fit the clamp.

If your Mini has been cared for and treated to regular oil and filter changes, there is every chance that a major overhaul will never be required in the life of the car. But it's not a perfect world, and you could face the prospect of a complete stripdown (which would definitely be on the cards if you are contemplating serious power tuning rather than a few minor tweaks).

Earlier in this chapter I detailed the methods of checking the condition of the rings and bores using a compression gauge, so at this stage you will have a clear idea of the position. Obviously, there is no means of accurately assessing the condition of the big-ends and main bearings without pulling the engine apart. However, you can make an extremely educated guess purely by driving the car at 30mph in top gear and then flooring the throttle. As I mentioned in the first chapter, worn big-ends will knock heavily (not to

The timing chain is one of the A-Series engine's few weak points. It can wear and then rattle, although it rarely snaps. An alternative is to fit a rubber-belt conversion *(referred to in the final chapter)*.

The conversion components: On the left is the rubber belt and sprockets, alongside the original chain set-up.

The new components are a straight fit, without any need for modification.

The job is completed by fitting the outer cover. Because the belt runs dry, oil leaks are eliminated.

There is no substitute for a valve spring compressor. But treat it with respect because if it slips, the collar can fly off at an alarming speed.

be confused with pinking at the top end, caused by poor fuel or over-advanced ignition).

Harder to detect is wear in the main bearings. When they are excessively worn they will rumble. But actually separating and recognizing that noise from the rest of the mechanical cacophony is not easy. But on a positive note, an engine tends to wear evenly, and if the big-ends are not complaining the mains are very likely to be in a similarly serviceable condition.

If your Mini is fitted with an oil pressure gauge you are in a far stronger position (fitting one to earlier models is a wise move). Remember, with the engine hot, the gauge should show at least 25psi at tickover. Rev it sharply and the needle should move swiftly up to a minimum of 50psi, but preferably in the region of 75psi, and stay there. The speed the needle moves is quite important because on a small engine, oil pressure builds up rapidly. Or rather it should do. If the needle is slow to reach its peak, either the bearings are worn or the oil pump needs replacing.

The basic rule of thumb when assessing the main components of your engine is to see whether it performs satisfactorily, does not knock or rumble and does not blow clouds of smoke from the exhaust (burning noticeable amounts of oil between services). If it passes these tests then all is well.

It may be as a result of some sort of mechanical masochistic tendency, but an engine which requires major attention is something which I relish rather than baulk at. Part of it is that I enjoy working on engines, and the other reason is that I enjoy even more the moment when a freshly built unit is fired up for the first time and it runs sweetly. However, a rebuild is not everybody's idea of fun and you might well consider buying an exchange engine.

Provided it comes from a reputable company, there is absolutely nothing against taking this route. In fact you might even save money, bearing in mind the cost of a rebore, crank regrinding, various other components and new gaskets. It's all a matter of personal preference, but whatever your approach, the engine will have to be removed.

There are two ways to do this, the first being to disconnect the subframe from the underside and then literally lift the body clear. It's one to consider, agreed, and an option that some mechanics prefer. However, I don't, for several reasons, not the least being that the suspension has to be disconnected, the engine, transmission and ancillaries are a hefty weight on the subframe and are, thus, extremely awkward to manoeuvre, and hoisting the body is a relatively delicate operation.

The other option is to lift the engine clear with a pukka hoist, and to me, this is unquestionably simpler. Obviously, the first job is to remove the bonnet. Not so obvious, however, is making provision for refitting it. Mark the hinges and where they meet the brackets so they can later be matched perfectly. A dab of paint is ideal. That will save you a great deal of time getting the bonnet to line up and close properly.

Now it's a case of working your way through each department. Drain the cooling system, disconnect fuel lines, hoses, cables and exhaust, remove the distributor and generator to avoid damage and then the radiator (technically untaxing, but incredibly awkward), the engine-to-bulkhead stabilizer (larger-engined Minis also have one from gearbox to underside) and gearchange linkage.

You'll need the car jacked up on the front subframe and supported with axle stands to tackle the underside. Remember, a jack is for lifting, and axle stands are for supporting. Never, ever trust a jack on its own.

Split the steering swivel joints, remove the track rod ends and disconnect the drive-shafts (see the chapter sections on suspension and steering, and transmission). Undo the engine mountings from inside each wheelarch. This is far preferable and considerably more convenient that trying to detach the mountings from the engine itself.

You can take several approaches when rigging up the engine to the hoist. Some owners prefer to use nylon webbing straps wrapped round the bellhousing and crankshaft pulley. Others use the time-honoured trick of welding rings to the bodies of old spark plugs to provide a means of attachment. I prefer using lifting hooks, which are held in place by the rocker cover bolts. You can either make them or buy a pair from a specialist. Such a set-up allows the engine to be lifted evenly and with little danger of tilting, which can have disastrous consequences to the bulkhead and windscreen scuttle.

When the engine is well clear, push the car out of the way and lower the unit to the ground. A stout piece of plywood of suitable size is ideal to work on at this stage. Remove the bellhousing, flywheel (with the correct puller) and clutch, then the flywheel housing (that's the aluminium casting which sits between the engine and the bellhousing). But before you do this, wrap masking tape round the primary gear to prevent the teeth damaging the oil seal. I would advocate fitting a new seal as a matter of course, so using tape for protection is particularly important on reassembly. You can now tackle the series of nuts holding the gearbox to the engine and separate the two.

If this seems to you that I am rushing through the stripdown procedure, let me reiterate that the purpose of this book is not to give a step-by-step, nut-by-nut account of dealing with the

Nothing beats the traditional method of grinding in valves, that is, using a stick and sucker.

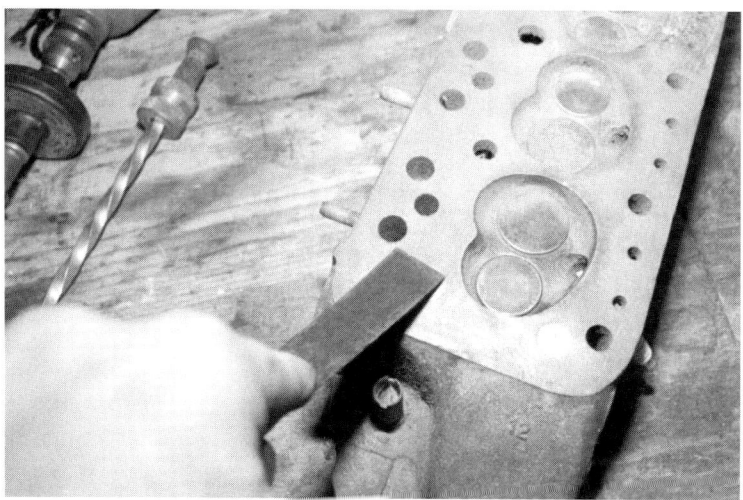

A blunt scraper should be used to remove all traces of old gasket from the cylinder head.

mechanicals, all of which will be found in a workshop manual. Let me just say that if you are logical, use common-sense and make notes of what came from where, I promise that you will encounter no mechanical horrors along the way. Everything will fall into place when you have digested these words and put them into practice.

Undo the big-end caps and mark each so that it can be reassembled with the conrod it came from. The same applies to the main bearing caps. Once the crankshaft is out, examine it carefully for scoring. Next examine the bearing shells. If the white metal has worn away to reveal any trace of the copper beneath they must be replaced.

Now comes the big question: do I just replace the bearing shells (and possibly the thrust bearings) or should the crank also be reground? Well, the crank needs a regrind if any of the journals has worn excessively or developed ovality. This can only be checked using a micrometer, and this instrument needs to be interpreted in skilled hands.

If you are in any doubt, have the crank journals checked by a specialist engine company. This is not a case of being a mechanical coward, just erring on the side of caution, the point being that gaining access to the big-ends and main bearings is a major job, and should you make a mistake you will be faced with carrying out the whole task again.

A well-worn cylinder bore will be evident by either a pronounced lip at the top of the bore or noticeable scoring. The same advice applies – if in doubt, have the bores checked by an expert using an internal micrometer.

Examine the pistons for obvious damage and burn marks, where hot gases have been allowed to pass by the rings. The gudgeon pins and small ends can be checked for vertical play by pushing and pulling on the pistons. No play is permissible.

In many ways, you will already have the answers because the engine would never have been stripped in the first place had there not been a problem, such as clouds of smoke in the exhaust or noisy bearings. Cleanliness is of paramount importance on reassembly because the tiniest piece of dirt or other foreign body can block an oilway and wreck an engine. This is especially so if you are having the block rebored or the crank reground.

Although a good engineering company will carry out the machining to the correct tolerances, the operator may not bother to clean off the inevitable swarf. So if you provide parts which are totally free from grease that swarf will have nothing to cling to. Even so, whatever part has been to the machine shop must be scrupulously washed in a proprietary cleaner before reassembly.

Big-end and main-bearing cap bolts theoretically can be re-used a number of times before they stretch beyond acceptable limits.

With the aid of a suitable hoist, and with the bonnet off, removing and replacing the engine is relatively simple.

Personally, however, I always fit new items because that removes any element of chance. Replace the main-bearing shells in the block, followed by the crank, then the other shells and caps (remembering to keep them in order).

Make sure all surfaces are copiously lubricated with clean engine oil. Tighten the bolts progressively and periodically turn the crank, feeling for tight spots. If the crank suddenly stiffens you know that one of the journals is oval or a shell bearing has not been fitted correctly. The crank should turn freely throughout the replacement procedure of the mains.

A piston ring clamp is needed to compress the rings so that the pistons can be inserted into the bores. This requires a degree of care because the rings are brittle and liable to snap. Lubricate each piston generously and then gradually tap it into its bore with the handle of a mallet. The clamp should be adjusted so that it fully compresses the rings, but not so tightly that it will not allow the piston to be tapped into place. It's a matter of care and patience.

When the engine has been assembled, turn the crank and again feel for tight spots. If new pistons and rings have been fitted, expect to feel firm resistance, which is normal and nothing to worry about provided the resistance is even and not suddenly pronounced.

The camshaft should be examined for wear. In fact, you probably won't get another opportunity to look at it because the shaft will not come out unless the engine is removed. I can almost guarantee that some of you will say that the shaft can be extracted without removing the engine and, to be honest, I have seen the job done by half-raising the engine from the body and/or cutting chunks of metal from the inner wing. But take my word, these are not practical ideas.

The cam lobes should be free from pitting, as should the followers. Unlike with the big-end and main-bearing journals, the amount of wear is not as critical as the discrepancies between each lobe. Provided each is within a few thousandths of an inch of the others you know that wear has been even and the camshaft is serviceable. If you're fitting a new camshaft always fit new followers. New and old do not mix well and the rate of wear will be alarming.

As you'll see in the transmission section, I am no great advocate of anybody but experienced and skilled mechanics rebuilding gearboxes, and I hold these views for several reasons. However, having got the 'box apart from the engine, you would be foolish not to examine the internals, looking for chipped or worn teeth. If, prior to the stripdown, the gearbox has provided reasonably smooth changes and none of the gears has slipped out of mesh or been excessively noisy then the 'box is fine. It's wise – although not vital – to clean the internals with a flushing oil to remove any impurities or foreign bodies.

At the flywheel end of the engine you will have encountered the idler gear, which links the engine and gearbox shafts. Considering the forces it deals with, this gear is remarkably long-lived. However, lack of regular oil changes, high mileages or sometimes just pure bad luck can take their toll, not so much on the gear, but the bearings in which it turns. Wear in either of the bearings will result in a transmission which 'sings' regardless of the gear selected. The noise is pronounced to the point of embarrassment, so you won't have any trouble making an early diagnosis.

Replacing the bearing in the gearbox casing requires a suitable puller and that's simple enough. An internal puller can also be used to remove the bearing in the flywheel housing, but this job can be extremely difficult and you often find that the bearing breaks up before it shifts.

There are two alternative methods, one favoured by some being to fill the bearing housing with grease, insert the idler gear shaft and sharply tap it home with a copper mallet. Grease cannot be compressed and thus it will force out the bearing. I have used this procedure with more successes than failures, but it isn't guaranteed to work, especially if the idler gear shaft is worn to the extent that it allows the grease to escape.

The other method is somewhat cruder, but generally effective. Heat the flywheel housing in an oven so that the aluminium expands enough to free the bearing. Now bang the housing edge on a piece of wood and the bearing should jolt free. Wear thick gloves to avoid burning yourself.

As for judging the temperature, heat the aluminium to the extent that spittle will bounce off it. A somewhat basic test, but one that is well-used and accurate.

The oil pump, of course, is vital to your engine and if you have had any reason to doubt its effectiveness – such as low oil pressure when the engine is hot or an oil pressure gauge needle which only slowly reaches its maximum reading rather than sweeping round the dial – replace it.

If I were carrying out a major rebuild of the bearings, crank, pistons and bores, there would be no quibbling – the pump would be replaced, too. Peace of mind is worth more than the price of a new pump.

The use of gasket compounds when rebuilding an engine is a somewhat vexed subject. Old-school mechanics will throw up their hands in disgust and say that care, cleanliness and new gaskets are all that you need. I can see their point because what can look more sloppy than an engine oozing jointing compound? The answer to that is an engine oozing oil.

There is no doubt that perfectly clean and flat surfaces which have been mated with new gaskets will not allow oil to escape. However, I can see absolutely no point in taking chances and I work on the theory that if components are extremely

There are two ways of removing the engine. One is to lower the subframe and then raise the body. The other is with a hoist and ropes, chains or nylon webbing, a method the author – like many other enthusiasts – prefers.

hard to access or are unlikely ever to be dismantled again, a jointing compound should be used. Then you know that leaks will not be a problem.

On the other hand, should you be mating parts which are easy to get at – the thermostat housing, for example – then a compound is unnecessary (but there are exceptions, such as the rocker cover – as explained earlier).

It's the care that counts when using the compound. Apply it sparingly with a small paint brush, using enough to effect a seal but not so much that it will squash out when the joint is tightened. If there is any chance that a compound can get into an oilway, the rule is simple – don't use it.

As you will have discovered when removing the engine from your Mini, the task was not so much technically difficult as time-consuming because some of the nuts and bolts were awkward to get at. Therefore, before replacing the engine, you can make life appreciably easier for yourself with the help of a welder. If you attach the nuts to the mountings with dabs of weld, thereby making them captive, they will remain in position when you insert the bolts from the inner wings. It will save you the hassle of trying to hold them in position while the bolts are fitted and it will also mean that there is no need to use a spanner on them.

One other non-technical, but nevertheless useful tip before refitting the engine is to thoroughly clean the engine bay with a degreasant. It won't make your Mini run any better, but working in a clean bay (with any rust spots treated and touched in) will provide a great psychological spur.

At this stage, a torque wrench will already be an integral part of your workshop armoury, and incredibly useful it is, too. But it would be unreasonable – not to mention repetitive almost to the point of boredom – to use it on every nut and bolt. For the most part, you will rely on pure 'feel' – that is, tightening a fastener just the right amount without overdoing the job.

But there will inevitably come a time which every mechanic dreads – when a nut or bolt tightens and then suddenly loses grip. That most unwelcome of visitors – the stripped thread. Of course, if it's a plain nut-and-bolt job passing through a bracket, for example, that's not a problem. It's when you are dealing with threaded holes in castings that the panic bells ring – not surprisingly because, on the face of it, the cure may look like a job for a professional. But whereas that was once the case, sorting out damaged internal threads is now well within the scope of the keen amateur.

Typical examples of candidates for wrecked threads are manifold studs, the thermostat housing fasteners and bolt holes for the timing chain cover. The solution is to fit a thread insert. Those in the know automatically refer to them as Helicoils. In fact, that's a trade name and there are several alternatives. Choose at will – provided you deal with a reputable specialist hardware store there won't be a problem.

The insert kit comprises the insert itself, fitting tool and thread tap. You'll need to buy the appropriate drill. The routine is to drill out the old thread, tap the hole and then screw in the insert. You'll get full instructions and the procedure is simple. I have used inserts many times and what was once something I was in awe of after reading technical publications has now become second nature.

Typically the insert is made from stainless steel and has a diamond-shaped cross-section so that it (a) screws into position and (b) provides its own internal thread. Such a repair is regarded as at least as strong if not stronger than the original thread. Put it this way, I've never had one pull out, even from aluminium.

An insert can be used to repair a damaged spark plug hole thread. But it's an expensive exercise because of the size of the drill and tap. And, of course, the head must be removed so that swarf doesn't get into the bore. If you're seriously into DIY it would be worth buying a complete range of inserts to cover the most common thread sizes on your Mini. It's ultimately cheaper for the long-term enthusiast.

A stripped thread can be repaired with an insert kit. First, drill out the hole slightly oversize.

The hole is now tapped to accept the insert.

The insert is screwed into place using the tool provided. It will accept an oversize bolt and be at least as strong as the original thread.

This tool is called a thread-chaser. It will clean up and reclaim a damaged thread in a spark plug hole.

35

Only a person who has carried out a complete stripdown and then re-installed the power unit, all connected up and ready to go, can fully appreciate the build-up of anticipation before the ignition key is turned. Without putting too fine an emotional point on enthusiasm for cars, it's an exciting moment. Well, just make a few final checks. The oil should be fully topped up, all hoses fitted and coolant added to the system. Naturally, the engine will need all the help it can get because with new rings and a rebore it will be tight. The battery should be fully charged and the ignition timing must be spot-on.

First, though, turn the engine over several times with the spark plugs removed to prime the oil pump so that none of the bearings runs dry. Even a few seconds without lubricant will do a significant amount of damage. Now fit the plugs, turn the key and your patience should be rewarded.

If the engine doesn't fire after a few minutes you need to make a few more checks. Basically, an engine will run provided it has compression, fuel-air mixture and sparks at the right time. A non-starter will almost certainly be suffering from an ignition problem (the favourite mistake, even for an experienced mechanic, is to get the firing order wrong) or lack of fuel (*see the ignition section of the electrical system chapter and the fuel system chapter*). But if you've rebuilt the engine with care and the distributor and carburettor have been replaced in the reverse order of removal, there should be nothing to prevent the engine from bursting into life.

Let it run for a couple of minutes and be prepared for stalling. New rings will hold back its progress for a short while before they initially bed in. The rings may also 'sing' in their bores for a few seconds. Now switch off, wait a couple of minutes and check the oil level on the dipstick. Start up again, let the engine idle for several minutes, switch off and check for oil and water leaks. There's a reasonably good chance that the mixture will now be out because the engine's breathing characteristics will be slightly different as a result of the rebuild. In other words, it will be working more efficiently. The symptoms will be a poor or erratic tickover or hesitation when the throttle is opened.

At this stage, don't worry because the carburettor will not need anything more than a minor adjustment, so no harm can be done. Until the engine has freed off a little, fiddling with the carb will be a waste of time. Once you're satisfied that the oil and coolant levels are correct – and are remaining that way – you're ready for the road. No doubt you have read much about running in an engine and seen advice on what speeds never to exceed in certain gears. Well, of course, that is sound practice. However, I've always run in engines using common-sense rather than set road speeds. It's not so much the mph which counts as the engine's revolutions and the load it is put under. The point being, for example, that you may not exceed 40mph in top gear, which is fine. But if you're trying to maintain that speed on a steep gradient the engine will be under strain.

So basically, just drive your Mini with respect, don't over-rev it and never labour it on a hill. You can tell by the engine note whether it is being stressed by too many rpm or being asked to work too hard in too high a gear. As for running-in periods, the big-end and main bearings will be comfortably settled in after 500 miles whereas new rings and a rebore will take 1000 miles before they have started to free up.

Therefore, with a full rebuild, you need at least 1000 careful miles of driving before the first oil and filter change. At this stage, you should also re-torque the cylinder head and check the tappet clearances. It's now that you can adjust the carburettor (if necessary) with a fair degree of accuracy. Slowly build up your speeds for a further 1000 miles – keeping a close eye on the temperature gauge – and that's it. Fully run in.

A belt-and-braces exercise it might be, but I would change the oil and filter again at 2000 miles. Then religiously repeat this exercise every 6000 miles and the engine will probably outlast the car, and your care, patience and diligence will have amply rewarded you over many years of motoring.

CHAPTER 4

Gearbox, clutch and transmission

Inspection, overhaul and jobs for the specialists

IT WAS the transmission layout, of course, which set the Mini apart from any other mass-production car when it was launched. For although front-wheel drive was by no means ground-breaking in 1959, the idea of a transverse-mounted engine on top of a gearbox, which incorporated the differential, certainly raised a few eyebrows among the old-school designers. And it is this very layout which makes some of the jobs on a Mini unique to the marque. However, I guarantee that, with one exception, there is no repair you won't be capable of carrying out.

So let's start with that one exception and immediately dispense with what could be perceived as the negative section of this chapter. I'm talking about the gearbox. Although I have successfully tackled several gearbox rebuilds, it's not a job that I would recommend the amateur to confront and there are several reasons for this.

For a start, the gearbox is the most difficult component on the Mini to access because the engine has to come out first. Therefore, if you don't get the rebuild right everything has to come apart once again.

Actually diagnosing a gearbox fault is not easy because an irritating whine or the tendency to jump out of gear could be caused by a variety of ailments. Stripping and reassembling the gearbox requires special tools, which you will probably find difficulty in sourcing.

With the gearbox apart, you need to accurately assess – rather than guess – the condition of components and decide exactly what requires replacing. Also, matters such as end-float are critical and are not open to negotiation. Even if you have correctly ascertained what needs replacing, you will find that the parts are not readily available – at least, not in comparison with components such as valves, pistons etc – unless you know exactly where to shop. Just try tracking down obscure bearings, shims of the correct sizes and detent springs and you will see exactly what I mean.

A gearbox specialist, on the other hand, will have all of the tools and knowledge at their disposal. So it comes as no surprise that I more than strongly recommend that a faulty 'box be professionally rebuilt or replaced with an exchange unit from a reputable company. Believe me, that is not a defeatist route, but a totally practical one.

Clutch removal and replacement is a far more pleasant task than on a rear-wheel-drive car, the reason being that you don't have to crawl beneath the vehicle and then wrestle with the weight of the gearbox.

First, does the clutch need replacing? The two basic faults you are likely to encounter are a slipping clutch or one that judders on take-up of drive. To check for slip, drive the car to 30mph in top gear and then floor the throttle. If the revs rise but the road speed doesn't then the clutch is slipping.

Before considering clutch removal, check that there is a working clearance between the clutch actuating arm and the locknut and bolt which act as a stop on the bellhousing. No clearance means the clutch cannot engage fully.

A slight judder is something you can probably live with (first, make sure that the stabilizer bar from engine to bulkhead is secure and that the rubbers aren't worn). But if it is violent then the clutch needs attention. The usual causes of juddering are either oil on the friction plate or a worn diaphragm spring.

Clutch removal is simple enough. Take off the bonnet and front grille to improve access, followed by the starter motor and clutch slave cylinder. Undo the engine mounting and it will be possible to jack up the engine enough to provide clearance for removal of the bellhousing and then the clutch assembly.

You'll need a pukka flywheel puller on earlier Minis because the clutch components sit each side of the flywheel. However, later models have the so-called Verto-type clutch and the pressure and friction plates bolt to the outside of the flywheel, as on most other cars.

A worn friction plate will be immediately apparent by the amount of material remaining. If it's anywhere near down to the rivets then you know that the item is no longer serviceable. The chances are that if it has been slipping for a while the rivets will have become exposed. This can score the flywheel and unless those scores are anything other than slight the surface will need skimming.

An oily friction plate means that the primary gear seal is faulty and this must be replaced. An easy enough job. In any event, always replace the three components of the clutch – the friction plate, the release bearing and the pressure plate. Naturally, the friction plate will be replaced anyway because this is the component which wears out first.

But wear in either the pressure plate or the release bearing will not be so obvious and it is tempting to refit the old items. The pressure plate, like so many other components on a car, beds in with its attendant part – in this case the friction plate – and to mix old and new is not advisable. You could well end up with even more judder than you started with. As for the release bearing, it's one of those parts which should be replaced as a matter of course because you then know for sure that it need not be disturbed again.

A couple of tips on fitting your new clutch: the pressure plate and diaphragm spring housing should each be clearly marked with the letter 'A'. These letters signify where each component is balanced and the letters should coincide on reassembly. Also, the friction plate will have one side marked 'Flywheel' and, of course, this should face that component.

That side of the plate has more friction material than the other for a very good purpose. Should matters get to the stage when you wear the plate down to the rivets, it's on the diaphragm side that the rivets will show through first. So when the clutch begins to slip, only the

If the clutch is slipping replace it as soon as possible; if the friction material is allowed to wear down to the rivets, you could score the flywheel.

diaphragm face can get scored and the flywheel will remain intact. That, of course, is the preferred situation because some owners allow clutch slip to continue for so long that both surfaces become scored.

While the flywheel is exposed, examine the teeth on the ring gear for damage. Theoretically, an engine will always stop in one of two positions – each is diametrically opposed to the other – so wear will manifest itself in those two places because that's where the starter motor will have engaged. Nevertheless, carefully check all of the teeth.

Slight burring can be relieved with a file. If any of the teeth has become damaged you will probably already be aware of this because occasionally the starter motor will have jammed. A badly damaged or chipped tooth will mean new ring gear and that has to be shrunk on by a specialist. A new clutch will need bedding in for 500-or-so miles. After this period, check the throw-out stop adjustment.

The Mini's clutch is operated hydraulically and there are two main components to consider – the slave and master cylinder. Either is liable to leak after a long period of service. The symptoms are the need to top up the master cylinder reservoir frequently, and dribbles of fluid, either around or behind the rubber dust cover on the slave cylinder or on the carpet beneath the clutch pedal. Also, you are liable to experience difficulty in engaging gear because of clutch drag.

Another good check is to get a friend to depress the clutch pedal and hold it down. Now watch the clutch actuating arm to see if it slowly sinks back to its original position, signifying that fluid is seeping past the rubber seals. It is quite practical to fit new rubber seals to either of the cylinders, but I never do that. Instead, new cylinders are always fitted, especially when dealing with the master.

Slave and master cylinders leak for a reason and it may be because one of the rubber seals has perished or become brittle. However, the bore of the cylinder may well be worn and you cannot detect that by eye. So is it worth taking the

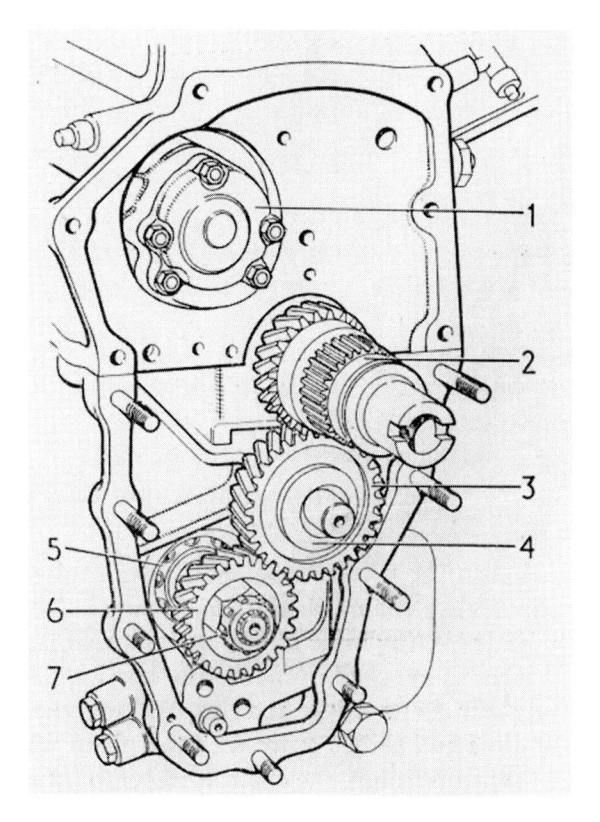

This diagram shows clearly the components exposed with the flywheel housing removed: 1 - oil pump; 2 - crankshaft primary gear; 3 - idler gear; 4 - idler gear thrust washer; 5 - first motion shaft bearing; 6 - first motion shaft driving gear; 7 - roller bearing.

chance? A definite 'no', in my view.

Removal of the slave cylinder is simplicity itself. However, the master cylinder requires patience because you need to get at the clevis pin which connects the pedal to pushrod under the dash. Larger-proportioned owners might find it easier if the front seat is removed.

Be careful not to let hydraulic fluid get on to the paintwork because it makes a remarkably efficient stripper. Always use new fluid for topping up and bleeding. The time-honoured method of using a bleeding tube – one end on the nipple and the other immersed in clean fluid in a clear jar – is as good as they come. You can then pump the pedal until fresh fluid goes into the jar without air bubbles. Do not over-tighten the nipple because it is fairly easy to shear. Just nip it up until it bites and give it about an eighth of a turn.

This is how a front stub-axle looks when removed from the car. By having it on the bench, work on the swivels or wheel bearings is greatly simplified.

Now we come to the drive-shafts and you will be dealing with one of two types. Earlier Minis use inner universal joints – also known as spider joints – whereas later models have sphere joints, enclosed in rubber.

At the road wheel end, drive is transmitted through constant-velocity (CV) joints, which have the considerably taxing job of not only transmitting drive to the wheels, but also maintaining that drive through various angles when the car is steered and the suspension deals with bumps. So it comes as no surprise that the outer CV joints can fail quite early on a hard-driven Mini. The classic sign is a distinct and ominous cracking sound when the car is driven on full steering lock.

Wear in either the inner universal joints or sphere joints (depending on the model) cause a thumping or drumming at various road speeds, not dissimilar to a drive-shaft being out of balance on a rear-wheel-drive car. If you suspect an outer CV joint then first examine the rubber gaiter. The chances are that it has split and been allowing grease out and the joint to run dry. A split gaiter is an MoT failure point so if you find that one of yours is damaged replace it – even if the CV joint is intact.

To get at the joint, you'll need to remove the drum or disc (depending on the type of brakes fitted) and the large centre nut is best loosened while the car is still on the ground. Then split the track-rod arm from its taper. Tap the hub from its splines and position it to one side, suitably supported so the flexible hydraulic hose is not damaged.

Split the top and bottom swivel joints (see the chapter on brakes, suspension and steering), pull off the swivel axle (or stub axle, as some prefer to call it) then the drive-shaft will be hanging free. With the earlier universal joints, remove two of the U-clamps so that the drive-shaft can be pulled clear, leaving the universal joint attached at the gearbox end. The later shaft with sphere joint must be prised from the differential. A special, wedge-shaped tool is available, but it is possible to pop it out with a small tyre lever, taking care not to damage the aluminium casting.

Be prepared to catch oil from the transmission. Have a container handy. Clamp the drive-shaft in a vice, remove the CV gaiter and then the CV itself can be detached with a sharp tap from a hammer. It's held on the shaft with an internal circlip.

Wash the components in petrol and check for wear. Having said that, if the joint was noisy then you already know that joint replacement is the

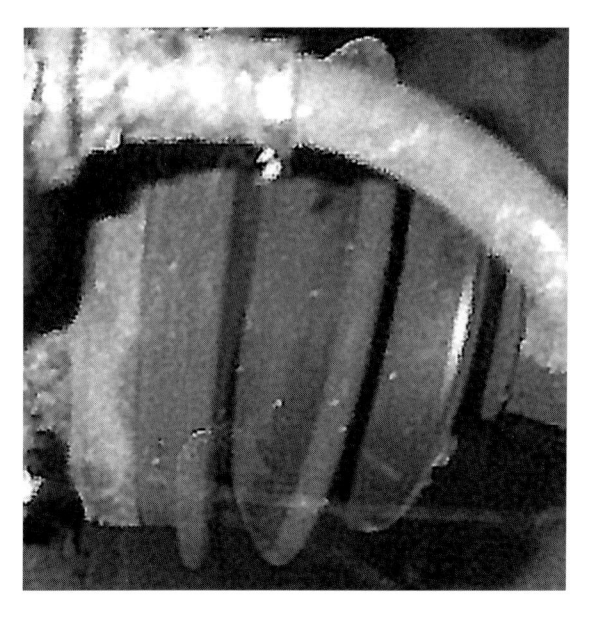

A split drive-shaft gaiter means that eventually the internals will suffer. It's also an MoT failure point, so be sure to examine each boot at every major service.

40

Wheel bearings must be drifted in progressively and squarely; a large socket makes an ideal drift. Similarly, oil seals must be driven home squarely to avoid damage.

answer. Similarly, the inner sphere joint should be replaced as a unit rather than attempting a repair.

The earlier inner universal joints can give many thousands of miles of service without problems and premature failure is usually caused by ignorance. The U-clamps which retain it are secured with self-locking nuts and the idea is to tighten them so that they are secure, but still allow the rubbers to rotate slightly within the clamps. This is necessary to take into account the up-and-down movement of the suspension.

If you do need to replace an inner universal joint, this can be achieved without disturbing the CV. The procedure is to split the upper and lower steering swivel joints, remove the universal joint U-clamps and then the brake drum (or disc); CV and drive-shaft can be pulled aside as one unit.

Cooper S Minis are a little more sophisticated and employ universal joints with tough, nylon-based cups with internal needle-rollers. Sophistication aside, removal and replacement is exactly the same.

At some stage, the wheel bearings will need attention and they neatly fit into the context of this chapter because – at least in the case of the front bearings – the jobs described involve the procedures necessary to gain access to the bearings.

The front wheel bearings are accessible with the hubs removed. Prise out the outer oil seal and then use a punch to drive out the bearing tracks. Take note if a spacer is fitted and also note which way round the bearings are fitted. Get them wrong and they will seize. On earlier models the inner faces will be marked 'thrust' and they should face each other, pointing towards the centre of the hub. Certain later models have lengthened inner races which butt against each other.

The front bearings have no adjustment because the wheels are driven rather than free-wheeling. However, adjustment can be made at the rear. The centre nut should be tightened so that there is a hint of play with hands at the quarter-to-three position on the wheel. Make sure that the bearings are packed with grease at every major service. The hub must be removed to replace the bearings and it should be possible to prise it off with levers or a pair of stout screwdrivers. If it's really stubborn, you will need a hub-puller.

Whenever replacing bearings, make sure that they are drifted into place squarely and all components are scrupulously clean and well lubricated with fresh grease. Finally, always fit new oil seals.

The front wheel bearings must be fitted the right way round, otherwise they will almost certainly seize. The inner races marked 'thrust' should face inwards and butt on to the spacer. On some later models, the inner races are lengthened and they should touch. To avoid problems, make a note of how the bearings came out.

CHAPTER 5

The cooling system

Diagnosing the fault can be more difficult than finding the cure

THE MINI has gained something of a reputation for being prone to overheating which, in my experience, is unfounded. In truth, the cooling system is no more likely to give trouble than on any other car. It's just that when it does overheat, it does so in a big way with potentially expensive consequences.

In fact, when you consider that the radiator is turned sideways, is in a confined space and does not benefit from a direct flow of air, you realize that the system is actually admirably efficient. Prevention is always better than cure and, as with any other area of the Mini, a few simple checks and maintenance tasks will go a tremendously long way to nipping problems in the bud.

On a note of caution – and this is vital – whatever you are doing, never remove the radiator cap while the engine is hot. The coolant is under pressure and it's highly likely that you will suffer scalding. Always give your Mini at least 10 minutes to cool down.

Check the coolant level once a week and then turn your attention to the hoses, gripping each firmly to check for perishing or cracking. Pay particular attention to the hose clip areas (a) to see that each clip is secure and (b) to satisfy yourself that the metal has not dug into the rubber.

Make sure that the radiator fins are not clogged, such as with leaves or mud, and give the fan belt a firm push to check the tension. It should deflect by about three-quarters of an inch midway along its longest run.

The anti-freeze should be changed once a year, regardless of mileage. When you understand exactly what it does, you will appreciate just how important this task is. Its foremost role, of course, is to stop the coolant freezing. Water has a most peculiar characteristic of expanding when it freezes – in fact, no other substance does that – and the expansion is so inexorable that it can even crack cast iron. In other words, the engine block.

The second job of anti-freeze is to prevent internal corrosion, which can quite literally stop the flow of coolant. It contains corrosion inhibitors to take care of that, and here it gets interesting. The inhibitors have a fixed life, and once they start to break down they work in reverse. In other words, they start to promote corrosion. In some cases they can speed up the process 10-fold. So change the anti-freeze once a year and that will never be a problem.

The proportion of anti-freeze to water is important because too little will have a negligible effect. Manufacturers recommend what the mix should be and, typically, you will be told to use 70 per cent water, 30 per cent anti-freeze. That is something of a compromise because the experts are agreed almost to a man that the absolute optimum is 50–50, regardless of the instructions on the container. It's a mix I always use, happy in

Adjustment of the fan belt is important to avoid slipping and, therefore, overheating. The alternator is held with self-locking nuts, which should not be over-tightened.

The heater assembly contains a matrix, just like the main radiator only smaller. They can develop leaks, which will manifest themselves as water droplets on the carpets.

the knowledge that the trade-off is a piffling amount of extra expense. So, in essence, the cooling system requires no more than a weekly visual inspection and a once-yearly change of anti-freeze.

By the way, when the cooling system has been drained and replenished, you might find that the heater no longer works; this will be the result of an air-lock. Simply warm up the engine, then remove the highest of the heater hoses until air bubbles disappear. But be careful not to burn yourself and, equally, be ready with a container and plenty of cloth to stop the coolant getting on to the bodywork – it makes a frighteningly efficient paint-stripper.

Curing overheating is more often than not an easy job. However, diagnosing the cause is where plenty of owners get flummoxed because there are so many reasons for an engine to run excessively hot. Let's bring the subject down to absolute basics and imagine a kettle on a gas stove. If there is not enough water in it – either because it was never filled properly in the first place or there is a leak – it will quickly get too hot. Alternatively, if the gas is too high the same thing will happen.

Now apply this thinking to your Mini. It will overheat through lack of coolant – either because the system needs topping up or is leaking. Equally, it will boil over if too much heat is being generated for the system to deal with. And that's the way you should approach your diagnostic session – first check for obvious leaks and if none is found, start investigating further.

Just a word of warning – and to save you unnecessary time and expense – if the temperature gauge indicates that there is a problem, but there are no other symptoms, such as loss of coolant, the tendency for the engine to run on when the ignition is turned off, a definite hissing sound from the radiator cap or cool air blowing from the heater, then suspect the gauge. These instruments rarely give trouble, but it is not unheard of.

Finding the cause of overheating requires a methodical approach and, as mentioned, you should initially check for leaks when the engine

It is important that the connections to the temperature sender gauge are clean. A poor connection could mean there is no reading. Alternatively, the gauge could give a false reading, suggesting that the engine is overheating.

has been fully warmed up. Likely culprits are the hoses (the bypass hose between block and head on earlier models can split), the thermostat housing gasket and the hot–cold valve on the left-hand side of the cylinder head.

This little device is wonderful in theory because, by pushing and pulling on the control knob on the dash, you have instant hot or cold air. However, this valve is noted – indeed, almost infamous – for leaking, the main reason being that it gets used only once or twice a year and the internals corrode. Some owners treat it with such mistrust that they absolutely refuse to use it, resorting instead to simply opening the windows in the summer. I am not quite that disdainful and do two things – give it a regular squirt with a maintenance spray and make sure that it is opened and closed at least once a week.

The one saving grace of this valve, however, is that it is totally accessible and, therefore, easy to replace. On virtually every other car, the hot–cold valve is integral with the heater and difficult to get at if, indeed, it is a replaceable item in the first place. Another component prone to leaks after a high mileage is the water pump. For the record,

this is a misnomer because it is not a pump but, in effect, an impeller. It does not force the coolant round under pressure, but pushes – or impels – it, just like a watermill only in reverse (the mill driving the stream rather than vice versa). Purely an academic point, I agree, but one worth making if only to top up your bank of knowledge for posterity. In the event I – like most others – still refer to it as the water pump.

The pump comprises two components, the body and the impeller spindle, with its blades. The spindle runs in crude, plain-metal bearings, and is surprisingly long-lived considering its technical simplicity. Its two biggest enemies are internal corrosion and an over-tightened fan belt, which strains the bearings. Check for leaks by running the engine at tickover and watching for drips of coolant. You might find that droplets are flung upwards by the fan.

If the water pump is simple, it is equally as kind to the home mechanic by offering a very definite clue to worn bearings – a pronounced shrieking, especially when accelerating, when the forces from the crank pulley and, therefore, the fanbelt are at their greatest. However, don't confuse this with the shriek given out by worn alternator bearings, which is almost identical.

Should the water pump be at fault, the noise will persist. If it is the alternator it will disappear after a minute or so when the battery has gained more charge and the strain on the generator bearings decreases *(see the charging system section of the next chapter)*. The other check on the water pump involves grasping the fan blades and rocking them to and fro to feel for play.

An extremely rare – but nevertheless possible – fault is a broken spindle, when the pump rotates and appears to operate correctly to all intents and purposes, whereas all that is happening is that the pulley is turning but the impeller is not. You will need to remove the fanbelt to check this. Turn the fan slowly and there should be slight resistance, indicating that the impeller is also rotating. In the final analysis, the ultimate test is to remove the pump for examination.

The radiator can be visually examined with the engine ticking over, as can its cap. The cap is spring-loaded and typically keeps the coolant at about 14psi. It is designed to open against spring tension should the pressure get excessive and act as a safety valve. If the spring weakens or the rubber washer perishes coolant will escape prematurely. If in doubt, replace the cap. The boiling point of water increases when it is under pressure – hence the spring-loaded cap.

Perhaps the most common cause of overheating – barring leaks – is a faulty thermostat. The housing is on the top of the cylinder head at the radiator end. Checking its operation means adopting the time-honoured method of immersing it in boiling water. It should open almost immediately, and just as importantly, remain open. So leave it under water for a few minutes. Conversely, a thermostat can jam open, which will cause your Mini to run too cool, which is harmful because an engine needs to reach its correct operating temperature for efficient running and to burn away harmful moisture which is a natural by-product of internal combustion.

Another potential leak point is the cylinder head gasket, and this might show up with a compression test on each of the cylinders. However, it is possible for the leak to be between a water jacket and an oil gallery, in which case your compression tester will not detect this.

But all is by no means lost and you should check for other symptoms which are: (a) water deposits from the exhaust tailpipe which do not clear when the engine is warm and which increase noticeably as the engine is revved; (b) a misfire on one or more of the cylinders; (c) mayonnaise-type sludge inside the rocker cover, which signifies that water has been mixing with oil; and (d) a seemingly inexplicable rise in the oil level, for the same reason.

Fitting a new head gasket has been explained *(refer back to the chapter on the engine)* as has the importance of fitting a new bypass hose, when applicable. You will have earlier checked the radiator for leaks. It must also be tested for internal flow, which requires nothing more than you would do with a domestic central heating radiator. In other words, feel it all over to see if it is uniformly hot. Cold spots mean that the coolant is not circulating.

At the same time you can reasonably accurately assess the flow of the rest of the system by feeling each hose in turn, which should be warm. If one is cold (when the engine is warm and the thermostat has opened) the coolant is not circulating as it should.

A radiator, like the rest of the system, can get blocked with internal corrosion and it is sometimes possible to clear it by back-flushing

Periodically check all the coolant hoses, looking for cracks or splits. Also, a hose which feels soft could implode and restrict coolant flow.

with a jet of water through the bottom hose stub until the water flows freely through the top union.

It is a pretty certain bet that if the radiator is clogged internally, then so too are the engine's waterways and, provided the corrosion is not extremely advanced, you can flush the whole system using chemical kits available at motor factors.

Typically, they come in three parts – a strong cleaning agent, a flushing agent and then a corrosion inhibitor. The cleaning agent is left in the system for a day or so and the flushing agent then comes into play. The whole system should be drained and replenished with the corrosion inhibitor. As I said, the success is entirely dependent on the extent of the internal corrosion and if you have just bought your Mini and know nothing of its service history then be prepared to fit a new radiator.

Luckily, the waterways in the engine are huge compared with those in the core of the radiator, which means that the engine is relatively easy to flush clean, which is just as well because fitting a new radiator is child's play in comparison to

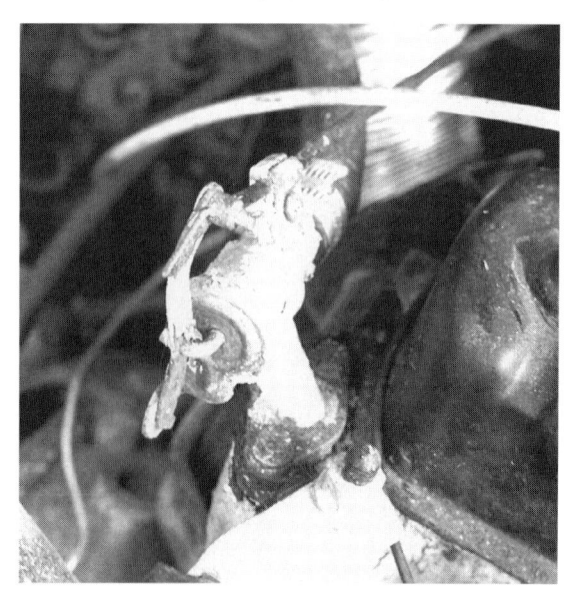

This valve on the left of the cylinder head controls the temperature inside the car. It is prone to leaking, mostly because it corrodes internally through lack of use. To avoid this, occasionally treat it to a squirt of maintenance spray and operate the knob inside the car.

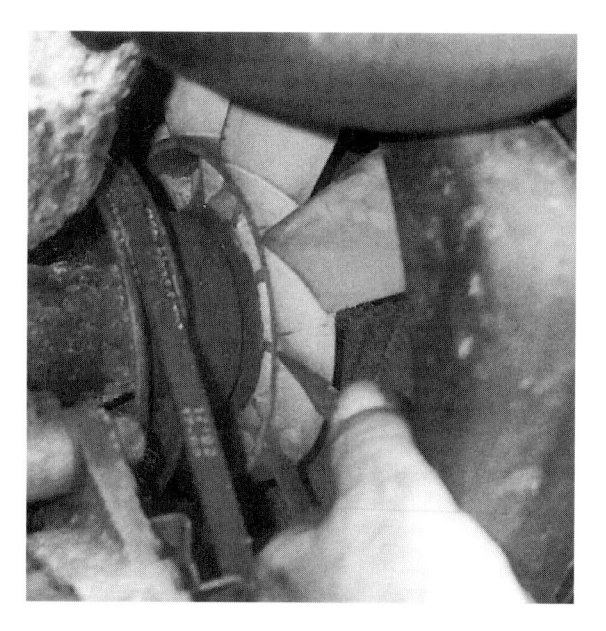

No play is permissible in the water pump bearings. Check by pushing and pulling on the fan blades. If there is play, the chances are that the pump will leak and will also screech when the engine is revved.

cleaning out severely blocked internal waterways. Restricted air flow through the radiator's matrix can cause overheating and this can easily be checked visually and rectified by blasting the radiator with either compressed air or a high-pressure water hose.

When dealing with a radiator I first make sure it is not leaking or the matrix is not restricted by dirt. If it has cold-spots and appears to be internally corroded, I back-flush it, and if in doubt, I fit new on the basis that the job is done, there is no uncertainty or guesswork left to cloud the issue and, after a fairly high mileage, a replacement is almost certainly imminent anyway.

You will recall that earlier I drew the analogy between your engine and a kettle on the stove and said that problems can be caused by too much heat being generated. Well, the engine will run at excessive temperatures if the ignition timing is severely retarded or the mixture is too weak. Both subjects are covered elsewhere in the relevant sections.

You may well have read in other publications that binding brakes can cause overheating because of undue strains being put on the engine. That

The fan and pulley must be removed to give access to the water pump.

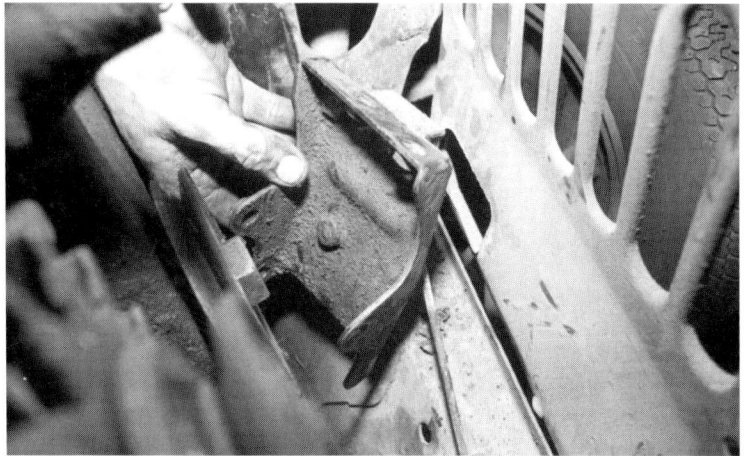

The bottom radiator mount is exceedingly difficult to reach. If you do need to remove it, make sure this component is in serviceable condition before replacement.

can happen in theory, but in the real world, if brakes are binding that badly you will also have experienced problems in the anchorage department, such as brake fade and the smell of friction material burning.

None of the jobs I have discussed – from fitting a thermostat to replacing the cylinder head gasket – is technically taxing because, as proffered, diagnosis is usually far more difficult than effecting a cure. In a nutshell, here, in order, is how I approach the problem of overheating:

1) Check coolant level
2) Check for obvious leaks
3) Check fan belt tension
4) Check water pump bearings
5) Check operation of thermostat
6) Check radiator for flow and also condition of the cap sealing washer
7) Feel each hose in turn to make sure it is warm and, therefore, the coolant is circulating
8) Check cylinder head gasket
9) Check/adjust ignition timing
10) Check/adjust mixture

There is one other fault which, because it is so obscure, has been left until last. This is an imploding hose. A water hose, just like a tyre, is a composite component, and although it might appear to be perfect from the outside, the inner section can break away and cause a restriction. This can be ascertained only with the hose removed.

In any event, always replace a hose when in doubt and avoid the wire clips, because they dig into the rubber and can cut right through. Far

If you need to remove the radiator, the cowling must first be unbolted.

Care must be taken when pulling the radiator clear because the matrix is extremely delicate.

Two types of hose clip are available – the wire type (right) and the worm-drive variety. The former should be avoided because the wire tends to dig into hoses and can cause leaks.

better are the worm-drive type, preferably in stainless steel to guard against corrosion. Also, choose the type with a hexagonal-nut fastener as well as the conventional screw slot as they can then be tackled using a small socket. A socket with a long extension bar is an absolute boon when dealing with that curse of Mini roadside breakdowns – changing the bottom hose.

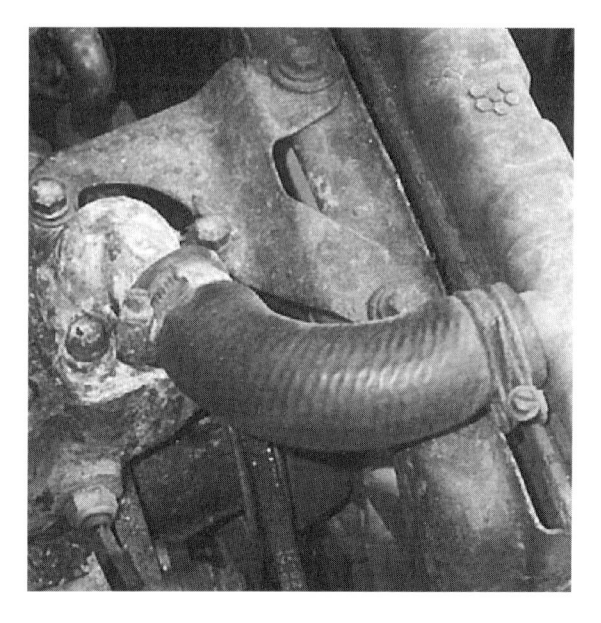

CHAPTER 6

The electrical system

Starter, charging and ignition systems and equipment

OVER THE years, I have rubbed shoulders with and worked alongside many talented mechanics (or technicians, as the modern world would have us describe them) and sometimes been amazed at their speed in diagnosing faults and their ability to cure them. But even some of the best fight shy of dealing with auto-electrical problems. And to be fair, electricity is something of a specialist subject in its own right and can confound the most logical of brains.

The biggest hurdle, of course, is that you cannot see it. A leaking gasket, a split drive-shaft gaiter or a maladjusted tappet, as examples, are entirely visible and, therefore, not too difficult to comprehend. But electricity is invisible, and all you can do is observe and measure its effects – a light bulb coming on, the starter motor turning, a voltage reading from a wire or, in the worst-case scenario, a shock if you touch the wrong component. In the briefest of terms, you rely on something happening to know that electricity is present and that the current is flowing. If something fails to happen, you must now decide whether the fault is electrical or mechanical.

Electricity can be broken down into three main components – volts, amps and ohms. Volts are the potential difference, that is, the amount of energy which is available should it be requested. That is the difference between the two terminals of your battery. The word potential is used to signify that this energy is potentially available if asked for. If this sounds like an exercise in blinding with science then think of it this way – a battery has 12 volts to offer, but unless called upon to perform, it will deliver nothing. However, the potential is there.

Amps signify the current, that is, the amount of power delivery – or the intensity, if you like – of the flow. Therefore, a low-voltage, but high-amperage (high current) circuit will give you a nasty shock, whereas relatively high volts, but low amps, will not.

Ohms are a measure of resistance and signify just how easy – or hard – it is for electricity to pass through a circuit. Think of electricity in terms of a bucket of water and a hosepipe. This might sound ludicrous, but the analogy will make sense once you have digested it.

The bucket holds a certain amount of water, all ready to deliver when requested (that's your battery). The hosepipe equates to the wire. If the bucket is upended and allowed to deliver at full force, an equal amount of water will appear with equal intensity at the other end of the hose (amps).

However, if you restrict the flow by squeezing the pipe, that will set up a resistance (ohms) and affect the characteristics of the power delivery. Try squeezing the end of a hosepipe and you will see that although the amount of water delivered is the same, the force of the jet increases.

In the case of a wire, it can be made deliberately thick (to reduce resistance) or thin (to increase it). A good example is the element of a heated rear window. It obviously needs to get hot so, by increasing the resistance, the electricity has a harder job to work its way through the circuit and, as a result, causes the element to increase in temperature.

This is by no means an attempt to explain in detail the intricacies of electricity, the subject of which has filled entire books. Rather, I have found that by grasping the rudimentaries, it has helped me diagnose and rectify faults. To put your minds at rest, you will need nothing more than a reasonable test meter (measuring volts, amps and ohms) – commonly referred to as an AVO meter, and a test light. And for the most part, you will deal purely with voltage.

The Mini's electrics fall into four main categories – the starter, the charging circuit, the ignition and the ancillaries (lights, indicators, heater blower, etc), and as mentioned above, the first task is to ascertain whether any fault is electrical or mechanical.

Starter
The Mini (like virtually every other car of the time) began life with an inertia-type starter motor. It's an electric motor (albeit an extremely powerful one) with a massive screw thread on its spindle which when turned throws out the bendix and toothed dog to the ring gear on the flywheel. When the engine fires and the starter stops spinning, the bendix automatically returns to its normal position.

In its favour, the inertia starter motor is simpler and cheaper to repair or replace. But the minus point is that it will begin spinning before the bendix engages with the flywheel ring gear, which can lead to the teeth becoming damaged.

Later Minis used the pre-engaged type (easy to identify because the motor carries the solenoid on its casing, piggy-back style). The huge advantage is that the starter motor cannot spin until the solenoid has first engaged the dog with the flywheel ring gear and, in theory, none of the teeth can get damaged. The trade-off is that it has more to go wrong with it and, therefore, is more expensive to replace.

Let's adopt the chronological approach and deal with the inertia type first. A common fault is that it simply refuses to turn the engine and a reasonable assumption is a flat battery. Turn on your headlights and try the starter again. If the lights dim noticeably, almost to the point of fading out, then that is the problem. That piece of advice may well rank in the insult stakes alongside checking that you have petrol in the tank if your car won't start. But dealing with basics is both wise and occasionally overlooked, even by the more knowledgeable.

If the starter motor shows absolutely no signs of life, connect a test meter to the terminal of the main cable of the starter and to the body (earth). Turn the ignition key to see if current is available. If it is, the starter is at fault and has almost certainly burned out.

Strip it down on your bench and you might find that the brushes have worn out. However, droplets of solder on the armature signify burning, and on balance I would fit a new component. Brushes last an age, and if they are worn the rest of the starter motor is in a similar state of repair. However, if current is not reaching the motor, the fault is in the circuitry of the main cable which runs from the battery. Check the connection at the battery and then at the solenoid. They might look good, but corrosion can baulk electricity to an amazing degree, so remove each connection and clean it with a small wire brush.

Now check the connection on the other side of the solenoid and that to the starter motor itself, repeating the cleaning exercise. A much smaller wire runs from the ignition switch to the solenoid and it is current from this which activates it. Use your meter to see if this wire is live when the ignition key is turned to the 'start' position. If not then the fault is either at the ignition switch or in this wire itself.

One simple way of testing the solenoid is to

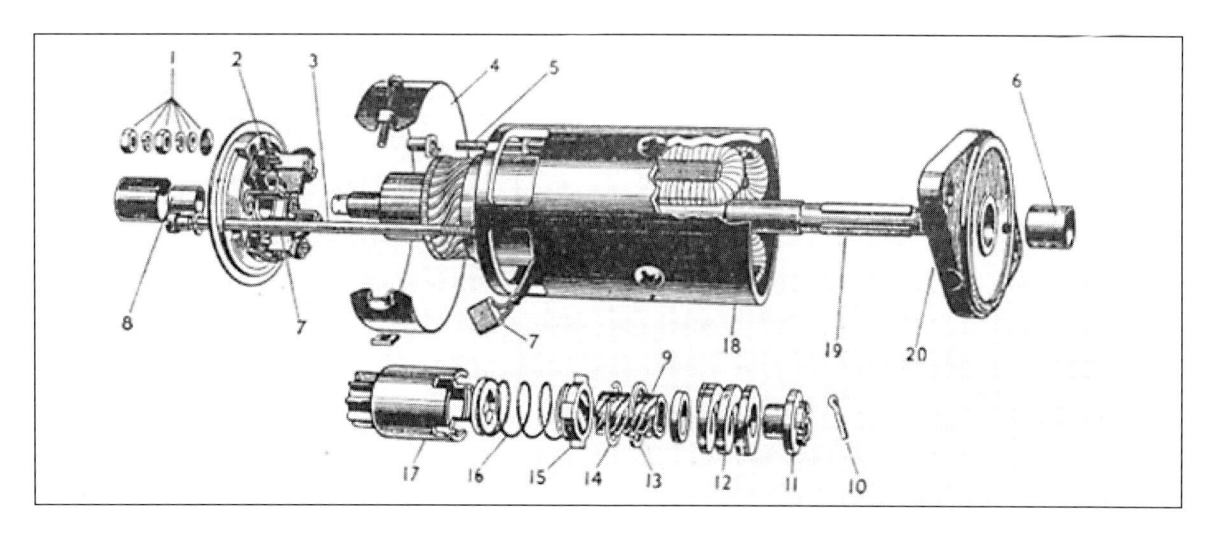

This is an exploded view of the inertia-type starter motor: 1 - terminal nuts and washers; 2 - brush spring; 3 - through bolt; 4 - cover band; 5 - terminal post; 6 - bearing bush; 7 - brushes; 8 - bearing bush; 9 - sleeve; 10 - split pin; 11 - shaft nut; 12 - main spring; 13 - retaining ring; 14 - washer; 15 - control nut; 16 - restraining spring; 17 - pinion and barrel; 18 - yoke; 19 - armature shaft; 20 - driving end bracket.

use a piece of stout wire to connect the two main terminals. If the starter springs into life you know that the solenoid is at fault (replacement) or it is not receiving current from the ignition switch. The switch is not serviceable and must be replaced. However, before doing that, check that all of the switch terminals are clean and securely connected.

Placing the Mini battery in the boot is a marvellous space-saving exercise. It also means that the main cable must run the entire length of the car to reach the solenoid, and a cable this long (and on the underside, at that) is wide open to damage. It can chafe through on the rear subframe, giving rise to all manner of mysterious faults.

I discovered this with a Cooper S and it took me an age to pinpoint the problem. The symptom was that the car would come to a dead halt almost every time I reversed. Intermittent faults are the hardest to diagnose, and credit for doing so on this occasion must go to a friend who spotted sparks from the underside of the car on a dark night. Sure enough, the cable was shorting on the subframe.

So why did it happen only in reverse? Because the suspension adopted the opposite attitude to that when accelerating forwards, and it was only then that the cable was jerked upwards enough for it to touch metal.

By now, you will have established whether current is reaching the starter and dealt with any problem in the wiring or with the solenoid. You could experience what is sometimes referred to as a lazy starter. That is, it turns the engine, but sluggishly. This could be a wiring fault and if so will almost certainly be the result of poor or dirty connections (poor connections put up resistance and impede the flow of electricity). Similarly, poor connections will allow the starter to spin, but not with enough vigour for it to engage with the flywheel ring gear. Once again, a check and clean-up of the connections will establish whether the fault is electrical.

One important check is on the engine-to-body earthing strap. If the connection is sub-standard, only a miserly amount of current will reach the starter. Is your choke cable stiff to operate or maybe jammed completely? That signifies a poorly-earthed engine; if the current cannot pass through the earthing strap it will take the next easiest route available and that is the choke cable. The result is that the inner cable and its guide will literally weld themselves together.

The other problem associated with the inertia-type starter motor is for it to spin and then lock solidly. That means that the teeth on the dog are damaged. If this situation goes unchecked, the ring gear will also become damaged. At this juncture, the starter needs to come off for examination. Damaged teeth on the dog mean replacement of the motor (you can replace the bendix or be safe and fit a new starter).

Check the teeth on the ring gear through the starter orifice. As explained earlier in the book, an engine will always stop in one of two places, so you need to examine the teeth and then turn the engine through 180 degrees to repeat the exercise. A small file will almost certainly be effective in dressing up damaged teeth to give you a good few thousand miles more of service.

A whirring starter – that is, one which turns vigorously, but fails to engage – is probably the victim of a dirty bendix. Because it is fairly close to the clutch, it can become contaminated with oil and then dust from the friction material, which prevents it from throwing out with inertia. The temptation is to oil it. Don't. The bendix should be washed in petrol so that it runs perfectly dry.

A final check on the starter motor is carried out with it off the car. Connect a cable from the battery (live side) to the main terminal and another to the starter motor's body. Now brush it over the battery earth terminal. If the starter is working correctly it will spin. Bear in mind that it will do so with a hefty kick, so be prepared for that.

All of the aforementioned also applies to the pre-engaged starter, except that it carries the solenoid on its casing, rather than in the engine compartment. The solenoid operates a fork which, in turn, pushes the toothed dog into mesh with the flywheel ring gear. Once it has meshed, the starter is allowed to turn. Hence the term pre-engaged.

Quite often, faults arise because of nothing more than poor connections and an ingress of dirt. Remove the solenoid, clean all of the components with petrol, lightly lubricate and reassemble. As with the inertia type, you can check the motor's operation with a few of pieces of wire. Connect the live side of the battery to the solenoid's main spade terminal and also to the connection for the thick cable. Earth the body and two things should happen – the solenoid should throw out and then the starter should spin.

To isolate the fault, bypass the solenoid by connecting straight to the main connection on the starter and earthing the body. If the motor fails to spin then it is at fault; if it *does* spin then the solenoid is to blame. In either case, I would forget about cutting corners and fit a new unit.

Whichever type of starter you are removing and refitting, do not over-tighten the retaining bolts. They should be cleaned with a wire brush and then lightly smeared with a copper-based grease. If they are too tight or allowed to corrode you could easily strip a thread in the flywheel housing. Similar care is needed when replacing the starter cables. The threaded terminals are delicate and it is all too easy to strip a thread or crack the insulation in the starter body. Also, as a precautionary measure, disconnect the battery before removing the main wire from the starter. This safety note has been mentioned elsewhere almost to the point of tedium, but this simple act can save an awful lot of problems, both to your Mini and yourself.

Charging system
If your battery is going to let you down, it is a better than even bet that it will happen at the most inconvenient time. A cold, damp morning seems to be its favourite moment. That, of course, is when it is asked to perform at its maximum – a cold engine with thick oil is always far more reluctant to start than when the motor is warm and the lubricant is flowing easily.

If it happens once and the problem disappears then it's probably because your Mini has been left standing for a while and the battery has not been given a fair chance to accumulate a charge. However, if the problem persists, you know that either the battery needs replacing or there is a fault in the charging system. So which is

The battery requires little maintenance. Just make sure the electrolyte level is kept above the plates and occasionally clean the terminals with a wire brush, protecting them afterwards with petroleum jelly.

it? Well, diagnosis means being methodical and eliminating each component in the circuit.

But first, a few brief words about maintenance. Once a week, check the electrolyte level in each cell. The plates should be covered, and if not they will overheat and buckle. Top up using de-ionized water. Plain tap water will cause the plates to fur up in much the same way that a steam iron will become clogged.

If you have the sealed-for-life type then, in theory, the electrolyte never needs topping up. I say in theory because the sealed type can lose electrolyte over a long period of time and that means prising off the cover and adding water.

The terminals should be scrupulously clean – use a small wire brush – and secure. At each major service, scrub up the terminals and connections, then protect them with petroleum jelly. A poor connection will set up considerable resistance in the starter motor circuit and it could just tip the balance from your Mini being an easy starter to a car which is annoyingly hesitant in firing up.

The fan belt tension must be checked – remember, it should deflect about three-quarters of an inch midway along the middle of its longest run under moderate finger pressure. Also, make sure that it is not split or frayed.

Low-mileage drivers should start and then warm up their Minis at least twice a week – preferably with a drive of a few miles. Engines and batteries do not like standing idle for long periods.

Checking the condition of your battery requires a few simple tests. It is at this stage that you have to turn your back on history. A decade or so back, a battery which lasted, say, three years was considered to have earned its keep. But times and technology have moved on immensely and it is by no means uncommon for a battery to last eight or more years provided the car is used regularly. So don't necessarily be swayed by age. It is the condition which counts.

Battery testers are available which give a reasonably accurate guide to condition. Typically, they have three coloured sectors – green, yellow and red. Green is fine, yellow doubtful and red signifies replacement. Personally I prefer to use a voltmeter. Disconnect the terminals and connect your meter. Even though the battery is rated at 12 volts, it should show an open voltage reading – that is, straight across the terminals with nothing else connected – of 14. If the reading is down – and it will almost certainly be in drops of 2 volts – then one or more cells is faulty, the point being that a 12-volt battery has six cells and each is capable of delivering 2 volts.

Batteries can be temperamental and show a healthy open voltage reading even if there is a faulty cell, so add a load to the system and repeat the test. In other words, reconnect the battery, connect your test meter and then operate the starter. You can expect to see the meter's needle sway violently, but it should show at least 8 volts. If the needle plummets close to zero and remains there while the starter is turning, the battery is highly suspect. It means that one or more of the cells is breaking down when asked to work hard.

It is just possible that the battery is in good order, but is gradually being drained when the car is idle by a short circuit. To check this, remove the main terminals and connect your voltmeter, carefully observing the reading. Now touch the two cables on their terminals and see if the reading drops. If the needle deflects noticeably you know there is a short in the system. This is a rare occurrence, which is just as well because tracing the fault means examining virtually every circuit and wire, especially looking for chafing where it passes through or close to the body.

Another way of checking the battery's condition is, of course, to have it tested by a garage. You have probably seen the meters the professionals use – two large handles and two metal prongs coupled to a gauge. This is by far the simplest method, so you must be asking why I did not mention it first. Well, there are three reasons: (1) because it is not always convenient to take your car to a garage; (2) if possible, and maybe because of a sheer stubborn streak, I prefer to carry out every job within my capabilities; and (3) I am a natural cynic and do not necessarily trust an emporium to test my battery when failure means they can sell me a new one.

Having said that, if you have built up a rapport with a garage then by all means take that route. If you need to buy a new battery, get the best you can afford and don't pick one simply because it is cheap and it fits. This is pure false economy.

Apart from having 12 volts of potential difference, every car battery is rated according to what it can deliver and for how long. The Mini battery varies from 30 amp-hour to 50 amp-hour, depending on the job it is expected to do. For instance, the battery on an 850cc model will be far less stressed than that on a 1275cc GT, which requires considerably more effort to turn over.

To get to grips with this method of rating, imagine you have one spotlight which demanded 30 amps to operate. Switch it on and it will remain lit for one hour with a 30 amp-hour battery. An extreme example, agreed, but if you compare a basic Mini with few accessories and a 1275 with halogen headlamps and a heated rear window you will begin to understand why the correct battery recommended for your particular model must be fitted.

One piece of equipment I used to employ, but now never bother with, is an hydrometer, which measures the specific gravity of the electrolyte and tells you whether it contains the correct proportion of acid. Modern batteries – and I am presumably right in assuming that yours is not the original and, therefore, has been replaced – do not lose acid unless they boil over. And once they have boiled, their usefulness is highly debatable.

Checking your battery, as mentioned, is simple and you will almost certainly be able to do it in less time than it has taken me to write about it. If it enjoys a healthy diagnosis, but still refuses to operate the starter properly, then the fault is in the charging system.

The Mini – like virtually every other production car of its era – started life with a

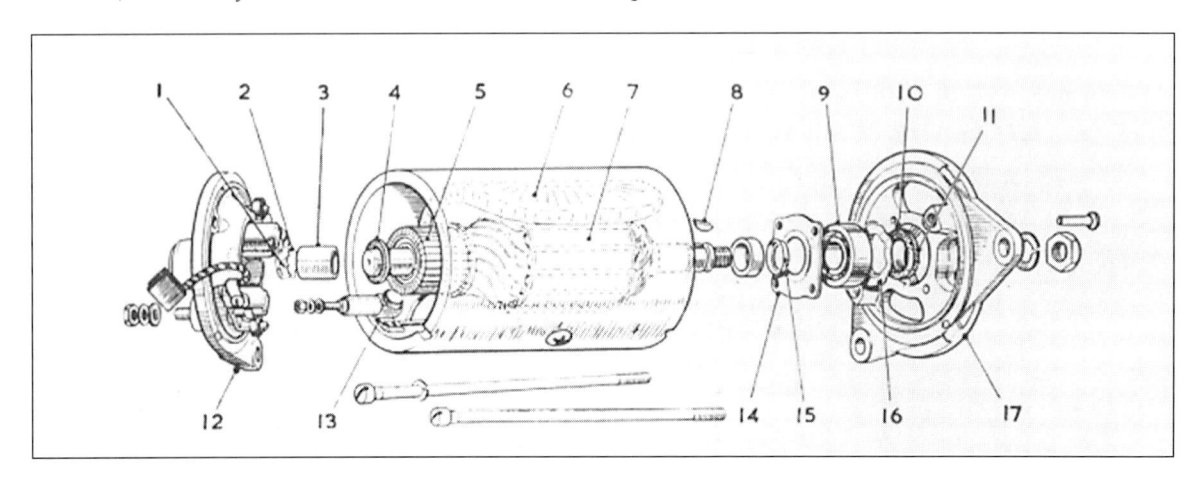

The main components of the dynamo: 1 - felt pad; 2 - aluminium disc; 3 - bronze bush; 4 - fibre washer; 5 - commutator; 6 - field coils; 7 - armature; 8 - shaft key; 9 - bearing; 10 - felt washer; 11 - oil-retaining washer; 12 commutator end bracket; 13 - field terminal post; 14 - bearing retaining plate; 15 - cup washer; 16 - corrugated washer; 17 - driving end bracket.

dynamo. Alternators came later. The dynamo is a mixed blessing. It is robust, cheap to buy and usually easy to repair (depending on the problem, of course). Its one main drawback is its lack of delivery. The charge produced is in direct relation to engine revolutions. In other words, the higher the revs, the greater the charge.

An adequate system provided your Mini is used regularly and is not overloaded with accessories, but add a pair of high-wattage spotlamps and confine your car to short, town journeys and a flat battery is a potential risk. If this is the case, use a charger every so often. The so-called 'intelligent' chargers now available are the best. They can be left on overnight, they sense when the battery has had enough and will switch off automatically.

In comparison to the dynamo, the alternator is far more efficient and delivers maximum output at little more than tickover. The drawback, apart from being more expensive, is that they are not really a DIY proposition to repair.

Whichever type of generator is fitted, you can make a basic check of the charging circuit without resorting to meters. First, warm up the engine to make sure it is easy to start a little later, for reasons which will be explained. Now put a large drain on the battery, such as switching on the headlights. Leave them on for a few minutes and start up (this is where the warm engine comes into play – it should fire immediately just in case you have flattened the battery too much). Rev up the engine and see if the headlights brighten noticeably. You can make a similar check by switching on the interior light and seeing if it also responds to engine revolutions.

Another method of checking is to similarly run down the battery and then connect a voltmeter across the terminals. Rev the engine and the needle should swing across, just like the action of an ammeter. A more controversial way of checking the charging system, because it must be said there are risks involved, is to let the engine idle and then disconnect the battery terminals. If the engine continues to run, charge is getting through. However, if you allow the engine to run

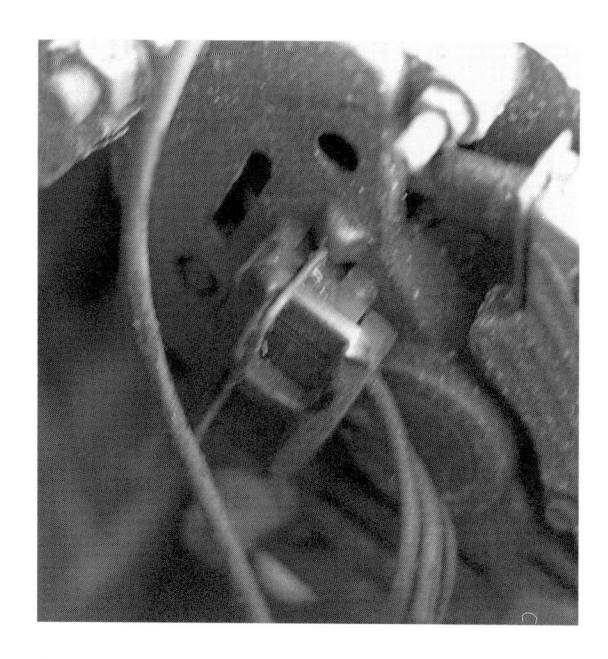

Periodically check the security of the alternator connector block; a poor connection will prevent the system from charging the battery.

without the battery for more than a few seconds, there is a chance that you can burn out the alternator. I have employed this method several times and never come to grief, but that may be a result of swift hands on the battery terminals or just pure good luck.

If no charge is reaching the battery the next steps depend on the type of generator fitted. An alternator relies on a live feed to excite the coils, so connect your test meter to the smaller of the two wires to check that current is flowing with the ignition on. If it is not you will have to trace the wire along its length and determine where the break is. However, if current is reaching the alternator, but there is still no charge, that component itself is faulty. You can have it bench-tested by a specialist, but the chances are that the findings will merely confirm your own suspicions.

The alternator, among other things, contains a diode pack to stop current draining back from the battery and a rectifier to change the current from AC to DC. It also has brushes. Kits are available to replace these components, but to be realistic, the success rate is somewhat hit-and-miss and I would always fit a new or exchange unit. The job is done, and although it could be perceived as wasting money, you have accomplished diagnosis by elimination.

Just to back-track for a moment, a specialist will check an alternator by feeding it with a live wire and then measuring the output at given revolutions. In my view, this component will either show a charge or not. Anything in between means that it is nearing the end of its useful life and should be replaced. This is a somewhat black-and-white approach, agreed, but such is the importance of a generator that I strongly believe there is no room for compromise. Adopt a similar approach and I promise you will quietly thank yourself – and maybe me – on a cold winter's morning.

Whereas all of the necessary components are contained in an alternator, the dynamo has an extra facet, namely the voltage control box (or cutout as it is commonly referred to). It's on the bulkhead and has a plastic cover, usually held in place with a wire clip. The dynamo's job is to produce the charge and the control box's job is to regulate it. When the battery demands a charge, the control box will allow it to flow via two solenoids. When the battery is satisfied, the solenoids operate and break the circuit, hence the expression cutout. So, in essence, you have two areas to deal with.

A dynamo can be bench-tested by a professional, but you can carry out virtually the same check by disconnecting the two wires and connecting a voltmeter to the terminals to check that current is flowing with the engine running.

There is another way, and this is more easily carried out by removing the dynamo. Connect the terminals to the battery and see if the dynamo motors – that is, spins. It is nothing more or less than an electric motor in reverse, so by introducing a current to its terminals it should rotate. Instead of outputting a charge, it is accepting one and spinning as a result.

Such a test should be carried out briefly to avoid burning out the windings. If it fails to spin, remove the end-plate and inspect the brushes. There should be at least a quarter-of-an-inch of carbon on each brush. Now examine the commutator to look for tell-tale signs of solder blobs, which indicate that it has overheated and the circuitry has broken down. Replace the brushes if necessary and run a hacksaw blade along the grooves of the commutator ring on which the brushes bear to clean them. Wash the assembly in petrol and, with luck, charging will be restored.

If you are convinced that the dynamo is doing its job then the cutout box is suspect. They are adjustable, but they leave the factory with the optimum setting and the chances of your getting it right are negligible. In the most pessimistic situation, the battery will receive too much charge and boil. A suspect voltage control unit must be replaced, and preferably with the solid-state type (no moving parts) now available.

Caution is one of my penchants and, because of the importance of the charging system and battery and the frustration they can cause, any doubt means replacement. On a similarly cautious note, never smoke or allow a naked flame near a battery because they produce highly explosive gases. And if you need to use a charger, make absolutely certain that the connections are the correct way round and that the charger is turned off at the mains before fitting or removing the leads.

Ignition system
Despite the advent, and now the almost universal use, of electronic ignition, many thousands of Minis are still soldiering on using contact breakers. But while this set-up can rightly be regarded as old-fashioned, it can be extremely reliable and, as a bonus, it is well within the scope of the DIY enthusiast to deal with. Fault diagnosis and remedies – not to mention roadside repairs in the event of a breakdown – should present you with no headaches. For the record, the Mini was treated to electronic ignition from 1990 and on 1275cc models only. That system will be dealt with a little later.

Points – or contact-breaker – ignition is my personal preference for the simplicity referred to.

It does require regular maintenance, but if carried out correctly, you will be rewarded with a first-time starter and excellent reliability. A good working understanding of how it operates will stand you in firm stead to deal with servicing and repairs, so let's trace it through from start to finish.

Turn on the ignition and a low-tension feed will run from the switch to the coil. The terminal will be marked 'SW', for switch, or with a plus or minus sign, depending on whether the car is positive or negative earth. For example, a negative-earth Mini uses the positive side of the battery as its live feed. In that case, the coil's terminal will be marked with a plus (live) sign. It is important that the coil is connected correctly because it will actually work with the connections reversed, but its efficiency will be significantly impaired.

The other connection on the coil will be marked 'CB' (for contact breakers) or with a plus or minus sign, depending on whether the car is negative or positive earth. For example, with a negative-earth Mini, the connection to the contact breakers should be marked with a minus sign. This wire runs to the distributor body and then to the contact breakers.

When they are closed, the circuit is complete and current is allowed to pass through the low-tension windings in the coil, which provides a build-up of energy. When the points open, the circuit is interrupted and the energy build-up is transferred inside the coil to the high-tension windings. It releases itself through the main HT lead from the coil to the distributor cap. From there, the current passes through a carbon brush inside to the rotor arm. As the arm rotates, the current is passed to the appropriate terminal inside the cap and then to the relevant HT lead, according to which plug is supposed to spark.

This all happens very quickly – thousands of times a minute, in fact – and with that sort of speed involved, there is bound to be a degree of electrical arcing between the contact breaker faces. Therefore, the distributor is fitted with a condenser. In the simplest of terms, this can be regarded as an electrical sponge. It absorbs excess current to keep arcing to a minimum, and when full will discharge itself harmlessly into the circuit, ready to begin absorbing all over again.

Obviously, the points must open at precisely the right moment – as each piston approaches top dead centre on its compression stroke – which is why the ignition timing is so important. Too far advanced and the engine will knock, too far retarded and it will lack power, overheat or backfire. Maybe all three.

Because of the nature of the internal combustion engine, the spark must be delivered earlier and earlier, depending on engine revolutions. An engine at high revs requires a spark fairly early for the combustion process to take place efficiently and completely. The distributor takes care of this with a set of internal bob-weights, which fly out under centrifugal forces as they spin and advance the ignition automatically.

A further piece of the jigsaw is the vacuum advance–retard unit on the side of the distributor. It's connected by a tube to the carburettor and, therefore, is subject to changes in depression, depending on the throttle position and engine

The base plate of the contact breakers must be free to move. Twist it in an anti-clockwise direction. If it is seized neither the bobweights inside the distributor nor vacuum advance-retard unit will be able to operate correctly.

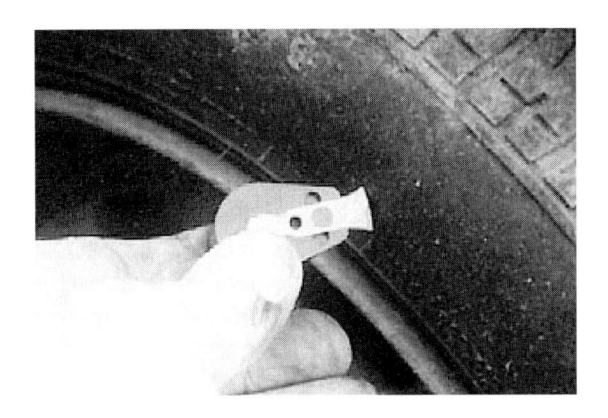

A quick and easy way to clean the rotor arm. The wall of the tyre will remove dirt without damaging the metal.

of a small mirror, such is their awkward location.

The timing depends on the model, of course, but let's say you need to set it at 5 degrees BTDC (before top dead centre). That means you need the pointer to coincide with the first mark after top dead centre. Turn the engine (plugs out, pulling the car forwards in fourth gear, or on an automatic, press the fan belt and turn the fan blades) to achieve this. The contact breakers should just be starting to open. Connecting a test lamp between the fixed contact breaker and a good earth will tell you this. The moment the light goes out, the points have opened and broken the timing. The smaller the gap, the more advanced the ignition becomes, so after refitting the points, check the timing. This can be done statically or with a strobe light, the latter being by far the more preferable method. In fact, on post-1976 models you have no choice because static values are not given for these models. The timing marks will either be on the flywheel – viewed through an inspection plate on the bellhousing – or on the timing cover, behind the crankshaft pulley. Their location will immediately become apparent on inspection.

With the flywheel type, the '1/4' mark indicates top dead centre and every other mark represents a 5-degree interval. The marks and pointer cannot be easily viewed without the aid

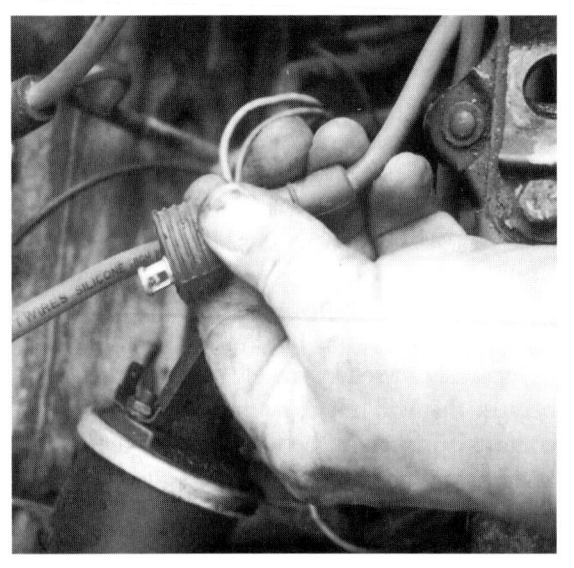

The main HT lead is attached to the coil with a push-in connector. It should be a secure fit. If not, just open up the metal slightly to give it better grip.

The low-tension connections to the coil should be clean and secure. When tightening the retaining nuts, be gentle because it is all too easy to break the plastic surround on the coil.

the circuit. The ignition obviously needs to be switched on for the current to flow.

Another way is to slacken the distributor body and turn it anti-clockwise slightly. Turn on the ignition and rotate the distributor very slowly in a clockwise direction until you hear a slight, but distinct crack as a spark at the points indicates that they have opened.

With a stroboscopic timing light, you must first clearly identify the pointer and appropriate timing mark with a dab of white paint or, even more conveniently, typist's correcting fluid, which dries almost immediately.

Disconnect the vacuum advance–retard unit to avoid getting a false reading and start the engine. The timing marks should be frozen by the light when they are exactly opposite each other. Twisting the distributor body in either direction will allow you to align the marks should it be necessary.

With the timing marks on the crank pulley and timing cover, the procedure is exactly the same except that each mark represents a timing variation of 4 degrees. In other words, two segments from top dead centre signifies 8 degrees of advance, and so on.

Whether you are setting the timing statically or with a strobe light, small adjustments can be made using the vernier screw on the side of the distributor body. The strobe can also be used to check the operation of the bob-weights and vacuum advance–retard unit. Observe the timing marks and then rev the engine suddenly. The marks should fly apart immediately, signifying the vacuum unit is doing its job. Maintain the revs and, as the depression drops in the inlet manifold, the timing marks should fall back to their normal position.

If there is no movement first check the tube from the carburettor to see if it is blocked. If that's all right, suck on it and see if the base plate of the points rotates slightly, which will tell you that the diaphragm is intact. Now disconnect the vacuum unit and increase the revs gradually. If the bob-weights are opening correctly the marks should move apart steadily and remain apart. If the marks

It's a tight squeeze, but you can use a strobe light on the crankshaft pulley to check the ignition timing. The scale (inset) gives a clear idea of how the marks are set out. The engine rotates clockwise, therefore the degree marks above the line are btdc.

do not move the bob-weights should be removed, cleaned, lightly lubricated and replaced.

Servicing an electronic ignition system is, predictably, far simpler because there are no contact breakers. Basically, the distributor relies on a reluctor to break the circuit (sometimes referred to as a chopper because it cuts through a beam) and an amplifier module to increase the intensity of the spark.

Because there are no parts coming into contact in the distributor, there is nothing to wear or to maintain. All you need do is regularly check the timing and make sure all connections are clean and secure. Electronic ignition rarely gives trouble but, on the minus side, it is harder to fault-diagnose and more expensive to repair. But as with most things in life, there is always some form of trade-off. Just bear in mind that electronic ignition deals with quite phenomenal voltages and great care must be exercised when touching any component with the engine running.

Some (but not many) Minis are fitted with a ballast resistor to aid starting, and to determine whether yours has such a device, look for a supplementary wiring harness incorporating a white/pink ballast resistor between the fuse block and low-tension terminal on the coil.

It works like this. The coil on this system is designed to operate with about 9 volts under normal running conditions. However, when the starter is turned, the normal circuit is bypassed and the coil receives a full 12 volts, meaning it is ultra-efficient. As soon as the engine fires and the starter is no longer spinning, the current is then redirected through the ballast resistor, which cuts it to 9 volts.

The idea is quite clever and works well. However, a fault can lead to a most peculiar situation which has baffled many owners, not only in the world of Minis. If the ballast resistor is faulty, the car will start quite normally, but then refuse to run once the key has been allowed to return to normal from the 'start' position. If you encounter this problem, disconnect the resistor from the coil and run a wire directly from the battery in its place, providing guaranteed current. If the engine runs properly then the resistor is at fault. Incidentally, but importantly, the coil in this system is precisely rated so it must be replaced with the correct item.

Statistics prove demonstrably that ignition problems are by far the most common cause of breakdowns, and I would wager than the vast majority of ignition problems are caused by lack of maintenance. So, if I am perceived as preaching, then take it in the spirit it was meant.

But even the most meticulously cared-for Mini can suffer from an ignition malady and you need to know how to pinpoint a fault. Your Mini will probably help you decide whether it is an ignition or fuel fault. Problems in the ignition department will almost always stop a car in its tracks, whereas a fault in the fuel system usually causes intermittent misfiring and jerking, ultimately (if you are unlucky) leading to a dead engine.

Let's take the worst-case scenario when either your Mini will not start or it dies in action. You need to work your way back along the line, starting at the spark plugs. Always keep a spare new plug handy. It will prove its worth. Connect it to an HT lead and hold the plug body against the engine block while the starter is operated, using a pair of insulated pliers.

If there is a healthy spark, repeat the exercise with another HT lead, just to ensure that current is reaching other parts of the distributor cap. Make sure that the points are opening and that current is reaching them (use a test meter). Also, examine the carbon brush inside the distributor cap and check the cap for signs of tracking. As mentioned, it can manifest itself as an almost invisible hairline crack. The rotor arm can also get damaged by tracking. I will assume that the points are operating (and the faces are clean) and all is well inside the distributor cap.

No spark at this stage has immediately pushed the problem – and therefore your investigation – further back to the coil. Check the connections and use a meter to make sure that the live feed is indeed live. If not, there is a fault in the wire from the ignition switch or in the switch itself. Provided current is reaching the coil, suspect that unit itself. You can have it checked by a specialist and play around measuring ohms for time immemorial. Far better – and simpler – to dispense with precise sciences and test it by making it do what it is supposed to.

Connect one side of the coil to earth and the other to the live side of the battery (the polarity was explained earlier) and you then know for sure that current is passing through the coil. Remove the main (central) lead from the HT cap and hold it close to the engine block with a pair of insulated pliers. Now brush the earth connection off and on the coil to simulate the action of the points opening and closing. The HT lead should provide a fat spark if held about a quarter-of-an-inch from the block.

There is a chance that the HT lead is at fault and this can be established by substituting a spare lead (or use one from a spark plug in the event of a roadside breakdown). As long as current is reaching and passing through the coil, the coil itself provides a spark, the contact breakers are opening and closing correctly and there is not a fault in the distributor cap, the car must run. If not, then quite simply you have missed something.

In some ways, a non-runner is easier to deal with than a Mini which displays a misfire or intermittent fault. At least you are dealing with an absolute – the car won't go, now it will. But with an intermittent fault, you can never quite be sure that it has been cured until after a fair few miles. But such are the vagaries of the internal combustion engine.

If your Mini is firing on three cylinders – typically, it will lack power, have an extremely slow throttle pick-up and an uneven exhaust note – the first move should be to determine which cylinder is not doing its job. Get the engine warm and allow it to tick over. Remove each plug lead in turn, using insulated pliers, to see which one makes no difference to engine speed. That is the faulty cylinder. Try a new spark plug and follow that up by using a substitute HT lead. If there is a good spark, at this stage I would carry out a compression test *(see the engine chapter)* to check the valves, etc. However, no spark means delving a little deeper into the ignition system. The most likely problem will be tracking in the distributor cap. Examine it internally for tiny cracks. One almost foolproof – yet delightfully simple – check on the cap and HT leads is to run the engine at about 2500rpm in the dark; do it at night or with the lights turned off in your garage. Any stray electricity will immediately show itself as small sparks or arcing. It will be bright enough to actually show through the body of the distributor cap.

A misfire or, indeed, one cylinder failing to fire completely can also be caused by another problem which falls most aptly into the 'why didn't I think of that?' category – a faulty radio suppressor. They can break down internally and leak current straight to earth, so you can imagine what happens with a faulty condenser connected to an ignition coil. As you will have gathered from elsewhere in this book, I occasionally adopt a black-and-white attitude to some jobs on the Mini and the ignition system falls into this category. That is to say, if there is a persistent misfire or poor starting, before attempting a diagnosis I would replace the plugs, points, condenser and HT leads as a matter of course. They are perishable items and, in my experience, shouldn't be trusted for much more than 20,000 miles anyway. You then know that these components are new and, theoretically, perfect and you can then concentrate on the other parts of the system.

By the same token, I never bother having a coil checked by a specialist who will tell you how well it is performing compared with what it should do. If it fails to produce a spark using the method described earlier, then in my view it must be replaced. It is extremely rare for a coil to give half-measures. It either works or it doesn't.

Dealing with electronic ignition, however, does not warrant such a brash attitude as far as the ignition amplifier module and the pick-up assembly in the distributor are concerned, because of their relative expense compared with points and condensers.

Connect a low-wattage bulb across the coil terminals and spin the engine on the starter. If it fails to flash the pick-up coil is almost certainly at fault. But first check the connections on the ignition amplifier module. If the pick-up coil is working correctly the amplifier module has failed. In reality, if the spark plugs are correctly maintained and the ignition system is kept clean and dry, you would have to be a very unlucky owner for electronic ignition to fail.

In the opening chapter of this book I promised honesty, and it is at this stage employed to its fullest when I advise owners to carry out basic tests on electronic ignition, but then to consult a diagnostic expert if a problem persists. Such an expert with the right equipment will swiftly trace an elusive fault which you or I might spend hours trying to pinpoint, maybe without success.

As you will almost certainly know, moisture is one of the biggest enemies of an ignition system, which is why the Mini eventually had a splash-guard fitted behind the front grille; it saves the distributor from a great deal of road spray.

Nevertheless, an ignition sealer is a great idea and it protects the distributor, HT leads and coil with a plastic film. Definitely recommended.

But what about the poor Mini in its earlier life, without a splash-guard? Well, any household goods shop holds the answer. The humble rubber kitchen glove makes the perfect protector. It's got four fingers and a thumb, one convenient protector for each of the HT leads to pass through, with the main section being pulled over the distributor and its cap. It was a popular dodge in the Sixties.

On a final – and mechanical rather than electrical – note, the distributor itself is robust and normally long-lived. However, the bearings can wear, and that can be checked by moving the spindle from side to side. A small amount of lateral play is permissible, but if it is significant you will need a new distributor body. Too much slop will cause erratic ignition timing and misfiring.

If you need to remove the distributor, make a note of where the rotor arm is pointing and don't turn the engine until it is replaced. Also, be careful not to over-tighten the clamp because it is not difficult to crush the distributor's aluminium body.

Other electrical equipment

If you want to give your brain a jolt and assault your powers of logic, study a Mini's wiring diagram. At first glance it will seem like a daunting mass of lines, symbols and small drawings representing various components, such as lights, indicators, horn, heater blower and so on. But study it more closely and it will gradually become apparent that the Mini's wiring system is not complicated, merely complex. Nothing is actually difficult when taken in isolation, just that there is a lot of it.

Having said that, I would never advocate poring over a wiring diagram just for the sake of it as that will only fog your comprehension. Instead, use it as a vital reference to trace a particular circuit whenever you are trying to pinpoint a fault. If, for example, the horn isn't working, then having checked the obvious – fuse and connections – you can examine the wiring diagram and then follow the circuit through from start to finish.

So far we have looked at the starting, charging and ignition systems. Now it's time to move on to the general electrics, and that takes in a whole array of components. They fall into the following main categories (not necessarily mentioned in order of their likelihood to cause problems): lights, indicators, horn, heater blower, windscreen wipers, radio (and tape player, if appropriate), fuel and temperature gauges and heated rear window (again, if appropriate).

I haven't forgotten the electric SU fuel pump fitted to earlier models, but that will be dealt with in the *fuel system* chapter.

The same approach to fault diagnosis applies to virtually every item mentioned – you have to decide whether a component itself is to blame or the problem is that current is not reaching it. This is the basis for dealing with any electrical malady. Which route you take depends heavily on the area being tackled. For instance, it's far more convenient to fit a new sidelight bulb than to check out the circuitry. On the other hand, if your heater blower has stopped working, testing the wiring first is infinitely easier than removing the motor for examination. With that in mind, the approach I advise will be dealt with as relevant.

First and foremost, if a system fails in its entirety – rather than just one part, such as an indicator bulb – make the fuses your first port of call. Fuse boxes vary, depending on the year of your Mini. In the early days, the manufacturers were content to leave it all up to a pair of 35amp fuses, later moving on to a four-fuse block and finally treating the Mini to no fewer than 24 fuses. A blown fuse is usually self-evident. Just look to see if the wire inside has burnt through. However, if in doubt use a circuit tester connected to its ends.

Corrosion can fur up the fuse holders, so check this out and occasionally treat the fuse box with a maintenance spray. Never fit a fuse of the

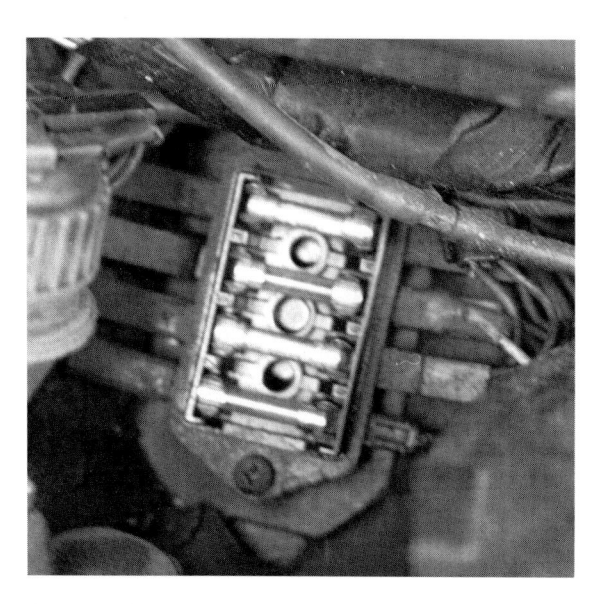

A variety of fuse boxes has been used on the Mini over the years. However, they are all pretty basic. Just make sure that the fuse block is clean and dry, and always replace fuses with those of the correct amperage.

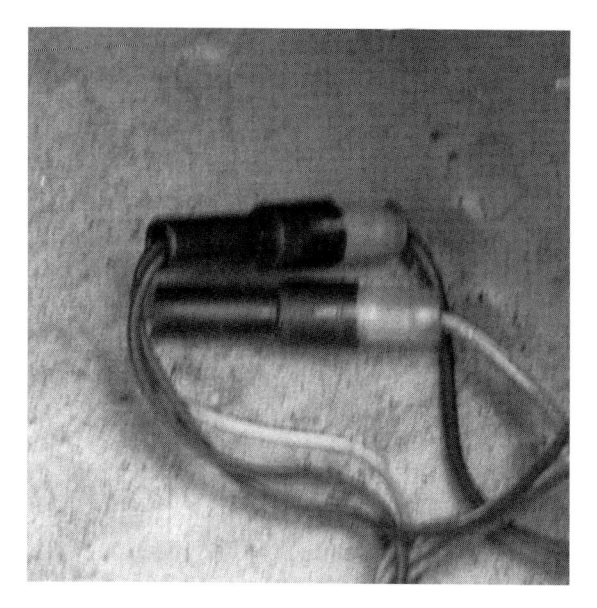

Bullet connectors are extensively used. If an electrical component stops working, check all connectors in the circuit. If in doubt, separate and clean them.

incorrect amperage. Too low a rating and it will keep blowing; too high and it will no longer protect the circuit.

I know that it's so easy and convenient to wrap tin foil round the body of a fuse as a temporary repair, but that is asking for trouble. It is human nature to forget that you've done that and a temporary bodge eventually leads to a permanent (or so you think) repair.

Imagine driving down the motorway in torrential rail and being surrounded by truck drivers whose sole intent appears to be cutting a swathe through anything in their path. Your windscreen wipers fail while you are in the middle lane. It is not a funny situation. I know, because it happened to me and was the result of a silver-foil repair to a fuse which had long since been forgotten. The foil corroded and all contact was lost. A salutary lesson indeed, believe me.

Moving back to more pleasant matters, the most common fault you are likely to encounter is a failed light and it is 99 per cent certain that, in the case of a front light, you need a new bulb. If a new bulb fails to light, you will have to trace the wiring back to the switch. Again it is an almost certain bet that a bullet connector will have

corroded, so clean it and use maintenance spray. However, if both sidelights fail to operate, suspect a faulty switch. Remove it from the dash and connect your test meter across the terminals to check that current is flowing as it should.

Matters are slightly different at the tail end because the bulbs press against spring-loaded

If a front indicator – or indeed any of the bulbs – fails to work and the bulb is OK, a test meter will immediately tell you if current is reaching the contact.

The engine must be earthed correctly, so check the connections. In this instance, the security of the bolt is doubly important because it also locates the engine stabilizer bar.

It is perfectly permissible to use the crimped type of connection for joining wires. However, they are subject to corrosion over the years so keep them clean and dry.

contacts in their holders. The contact should be clean and the plastic contact holder should move freely on its spring. Scraping the metal with a small knife and then using maintenance spray should sort that out. If it doesn't, use your test meter to make sure current is reaching the holder and, once again, trace the circuit back, paying particular attention to bullet connectors.

However, if current is reaching the contact the problem is a poor earth – an extremely common situation. Take out the complete assembly, clean it and ensure that none of the fixing bolts is corroded so that good metal-to-metal contact is being made.

Let us confront a real poser. You have checked and established that the fuses, switch, bulbs, earth and bulb holders are all in perfect condition, but a pair of lights – either front or rear – simply refuses to work. This can only mean there is a breakdown in the loom, and locating it is a virtual impossibility. However, the answer is delightfully simple – study the wiring diagram and determine which wire runs where. Now make up your own sub-loom and bypass the original, preferably using the same colours as per the wiring diagram. That piece of advice holds good for any electrical component which fails to operate and defies logic.

Your indicators should flash between 60 and 120 times a minute, and those somewhat incomprehensible parameters are laid down in the official MoT test rules. Far simpler to view it that they should flash once or twice a second. If a bulb doesn't work, replace it and, at the same time, check and clean the spring-loaded contact plate and make sure that the earth connection is sound. A poor earth often causes an indicator bulb to glow in unison with a tail light. Basically, they are both fighting for the same earth connection and each glows as a compromise. Total failure means the flasher unit needs replacing or the indicator switch is at fault. Remove it from the steering column and carefully check all of the connections and wires. If your indicators illuminate, but fail to flash, either the wrong flasher unit has been fitted or a bulb of the wrong rating has been used. Flasher units depend on current drain to operate, and if the bulb is not demanding enough the unit will not work.

As an aside – and it's a useful tip – you might find that the flasher unit does not operate with a noticeable 'click' which, although not a desperate

Removing the steering column shroud reveals the indicator switch and main-dip beam control. Generally speaking, this assembly is not serviceable and must be replaced if there is a fault.

situation, means you no longer have an audible warning that your indicators have not cancelled. Wrap the unit in thick tin foil, and the resonance created will make the sound of its operation far more pronounced.

Something else worth noting is that replacing the orange glass lens on a front indicator has flummoxed and frustrated many Mini owners. Fit it in the following sequence – lens to rubber and then chrome surround into the rubber flange. Try to do it in reverse order and, I promise, you will find the job is a physical impossibility.

All of the aforementioned checks and cures apply equally to a faulty stop lamp except that they depend on a separate switch. On earlier models, this is operated hydraulically and you will find it on the left-hand side of the engine compartment (viewed from the front), just above the flywheel housing and near the brake master cylinder. To check the switch, turn on the ignition, remove the wires and join them. If the stop lamps come on the switch needs replacing. It is not serviceable. Later models have the stop lamp switch adjoining the brake pedal, under the dash. Again, disconnect the wires and join them to bypass the switch to see if the lights operate.

Dealing with headlights is different because a sealed-beam unit or bulb are not cheap in relative terms and there is nothing to be gained from fitting a new item in the hope that it will work, except as an exercise in wasting time and money. If you suspect a sealed-beam headlight or bulb, simply connect it straight to the battery.

With halogen bulbs – identified by a matt-grey tip – be careful not to touch the glass. The natural oils in your hand will leave deposits and cause the bulb to burn out extremely quickly. New bulbs come with a sponge or cardboard sleeve to protect the glass. Use clean cloth when dealing with a bulb already fitted. A complete failure in operation of either the dipped or main beam will almost certainly be caused by a break in the circuit to the switch or the switch itself.

When replacing a bulb in its holder – that is, for front and rear indicators, or tail and stop lamps – you may well find that the bulb has become corroded in place and it is not unusual for the glass to break when you try to remove it. You can save yourself injury from the jagged ends by inserting a cork and twisting the remains of the bulb.

An inoperative interior light is an all too

This is a halogen headlight, as opposed to the sealed-beam type. Never touch the glass with your bare fingers because the natural oils in your skin will cause the bulb to fail extremely quickly.

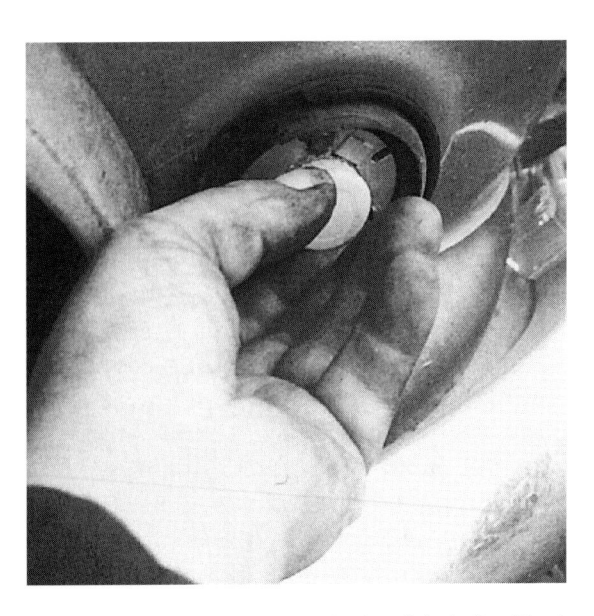

A simple dodge for removing a broken light bulb without cutting your fingers – use a cork.

common problem. Provided the long, festoon bulb is OK, remove and thoroughly clean each door-operated micro-switch and its connection and use maintenance spray to restore the spring-loaded action.

The horn – or warning instrument to be pedantic – rarely gives trouble. If it fails to operate, connect it directly to the battery. Adjustment is available by loosening the locknut and turning the screw in either direction until the horn sounds. No noise means replacement, but should the horn work, suspect the hooter button or – more likely – the metal slip-ring underneath the steering wheel. It and its contact should be clean.

Similarly, the heater blower is usually a troublefree character and failure usually means the motor has burnt out. First, make sure that current is reaching the connections, then remove the switch and use a test meter to check its operation.

Although the motor is not, in theory, a serviceable item, it is sometimes possible to work a few wonders with patience. Remove the assembly from your car, then strip down the motor. There is just a chance that the bearings are partially seized, in which case they can be freed using oil and then letting the motor run, connected directly to the battery. This exercise, if you are lucky, will remove corrosion on the bearing tracks. However, if the motor persists in struggling to turn, you know that replacement is the answer.

The windscreen wipers – like the heater blower – are a mix of electrical and mechanical items. Failure to operate involves all of the previously mentioned checks on the fuse, wiring and switch to establish that current is flowing. If it is, the motor is almost certainly at fault. A strip-down and thorough clean might effect a cure (as indeed, it should cure the tendency for wipers to fail to self-park). But in all probability it won't. Bearing in mind that, probably unfairly, a wiper motor is expected to last the life of the car, you will realize just how reliable this component is and can, perhaps, forgive the odd one for failure after 10 years or so. On a mechanical rather than electrical note, the spindles on which the wipers sweep to and fro are subject to wear and, typically, they will self-park halfway up the screen. Backlash cannot be cured and a new spindle will have to be fitted.

A radio (and tape player, if appropriate) which fails to work is easily dealt with. If the fuse is intact and the body is earthed the unit itself is the problem, and that is beyond the DIY enthusiast to repair. However, poor reception or interference are generally simple to cure. The aerial must make good contact with wherever it is fitted – usually on the front wing – so ensure that the clamping bracket is clean, as should be the attendant metal. You will find that many radios have an aerial trimmer – a small screw on the back of the set – and it's a case of tuning into the weakest station and then twisting the screw either way until the best reception is obtained. Interference is a nuisance rather than a major problem, but it is something you need not put up with. A suppressor should be fitted to the coil as a matter of course and modern plug leads will take care of the rest of the ignition system.

To check that these measures have been effective, remove the aerial and run the engine. A whine from the radio means something is amiss, probably a faulty suppressor or plug leads which aren't doing their job. Replace them. Now operate the windscreen wipers and listen for interference which coincides with their action. Once again, a suppressor on the motor will take care of that.

The world of electronics has largely been rationalized over the years, as a result of which all cars are negative-earth, as are tape and CD players, which obviously will pose a problem for the owner of a positive-earth Mini. Well, there are two solutions. Either buy a polarity converter, available from specialists, or wire up the player independently of the ignition, but isolate the body. This means connecting the set to negative-earth and making absolutely sure that the body cannot come into contact with any part of your Mini – a neat and carefully-made wooden box is fine for this – because a set will immediately burn out if exposed to the incorrect polarity.

The fuel and temperature gauges are quickly checked. If the temperature gauge fails to work, disconnect the wires from the sender unit, found by the thermostat housing, and join them. The gauge should immediately indicate 'maximum'. If it does, it is fine and the sender unit is faulty, but if the gauge fails to respond, the gauge itself is to blame.

Similarly, you can check the operation of the fuel gauge by removing the wires from the sender unit on the side of the tank, joining them and observing the needle. An immediate 'maximum' reading means the gauge is operable, which will almost certainly be the case (gauges rarely fail). That means fitting a new sender unit.

It is possible to check the sender by measuring current and resistance, but if it is playing up replacement is the answer. If you do fit a new sender, check its accuracy by filling the tank, when of course the gauge should show 'maximum'. Erratic readings from both gauges are caused by a faulty voltage stabilizer unit. It will be found behind the dash and looks similar to an indicator unit. Its job is to absorb voltage surges and thus give gauges a uniform reading, rather than let the needles flicker at will.

A heated rear window is guarded by a large-

All of the dashboard switches are easy to access on the Mini. Just pop them out using a screwdriver. The connections are then exposed should you need to carry out checks with a test meter.

amperage fuse or relay. The chances of the element breaking down are minimal, so failure to operate will almost certainly be caused by a blown fuse or faulty relay. As a last resort, make an extremely careful inspection of the element in the screen. In the unlikely event of there being a break a new screen must be fitted. Alternatively, fit an aftermarket screen heater, which has a self-adhesive surface.

Failure of the reversing lights will usually be the result of a faulty or maladjusted switch, which is on the gearchange's remote-control housing. Jack up and support the car. Now unscrew the locknut and, with the ignition switched on and reverse gear selected, screw in the switch until the lights come on. Screw it in a further quarter of a turn and tighten the locknut. If this doesn't work, disconnect the wires and join them; this will tell you whether the switch is faulty.

So really, electrical problems are all a question of logic. Is the current flowing? If not, why not? And if it is, what's wrong with the component it is serving?

CHAPTER 7

Brakes, suspension and steering

Inspection, adjustment and replacement

Brakes

OVER THE years, the Mini's brakes have been treated to several upgrades, notably the introduction of discs at the front on later models (although the Cooper variants had them well in advance of the rest), but progress doesn't mean complications because everything – from adjustment to a complete overhaul – is easily within your scope.

First, though, let's look at the faults you are likely to encounter and how to diagnose them. A steering bias when you depress the pedal – as opposed to the tendency to wander regardless of whether the brakes are applied – almost invariably means that one of the front brakes is below par. If the car pulls to the left, the right-hand side is at fault and vice versa.

The more knowledgeable among you will immediately proclaim that a bias could be caused by maladjusted tracking or an under-inflated tyre. In both cases, a sharp dab on the pedal will accentuate the problem and give the impression that the brakes are the culprit.

Agreed, those are possibilities, but I've got to assume that you keep your tyres at the correct pressures and that you also regularly check the tread patterns, bearing in mind that if the tracking is out, one or both of the front tyres will have a noticeably worn patch over part of its circumference. Quite apart from that, it's the belt-and-braces side to my personality which would make me instinctively first turn my attention to the brakes, the point being that even if they are not at fault, an inspection will not go amiss.

The Mini had front drum brakes for a surprisingly long period of its production life, relying on them long after most other marques had gone over to discs. Quite why is somewhat beyond me because the disc set-up is superior in just about every respect. But whatever the thinking behind the decision to retain them, if you've got drums you will have to put up with their vagaries (unless you convert to discs with the components from a later model).

Fortunately, with careful maintenance and adjustment, the drum set-up can work well. The biggest drawback compared with discs is the tendency for brake fade under hard use, when the drums expand with heat and effectively pull away from the linings, albeit to a small degree. In an extreme case, the pedal will go to the floor with no other result than to cause you a heart-stopping shock. But to put matters into perspective, that would be likely to happen only if you were driving to the absolute limit and using the brakes perpetually. In the real world, brake fade is something you are unlikely to encounter.

If the earlier Minis were destined to rely on drums at the front, at least the makers had the good grace to use a twin-leading shoe

Originally, only Cooper variants of the Mini had disc brakes, although later they became standard on all models and of course are superior to the drum variety.

arrangement, that is, each shoe is actuated by its own cylinder so that both expand simultaneously.

To explain matters, the term leading shoe refers to that end of the lining which comes into contact with the drum first. The rotation of the drum makes the shoe dig in and gives a self-servo effect. Therefore, with two pistons in action at the same time, both shoes have a leading edge (a vast improvement over the single-leader arrangement used until the mid-Sixties on most other cars, which was considerably less efficient).

First, you have to remove the front drum for an inspection and the square-headed adjusters need to be slackened. Use a spanner which fits perfectly (either a small adjustable or a pukka brake spanner). Unfortunately, it is a reasonable bet that one of the adjusters will have seized, in which case you should be able to free it with a pair of self-locking grips (sorting out a badly seized adjuster is dealt with a little later).

Remove the two retaining screws and pull the drum clear. It may be stubborn to shift, especially if one of the adjusters cannot be budged or the linings have been allowed to wear a ridge internally. If that's the case, sharply tap the outside diameter with a copper-faced mallet and you should be able to gradually ease it off by working your way round the drum.

Inefficient operation will be caused by one of three factors – poor adjustment, worn linings or a leaking wheel cylinder. The latter should be pretty obvious because the linings will have

Wheel cylinders are relatively cheap, so if one leaks replace it rather than fit new seals. That removes any element of chance.

When working on a component in the braking system – such as replacing a wheel cylinder – you can minimize fluid loss by using a plastic bag to seal the master cylinder. The bag comes free, at a supermarket near you!

71

become contaminated with hydraulic fluid. To double-check, peel back the rubber dust covers on each cylinder and look for weeping. Don't waste your time fitting replacement seals. A new wheel cylinder is cheap and, when fitted, you can rest assured that the leak will have been cured.

To remove a wheel cylinder, the brake shoes must first come off. Prise the shoes from each cylinder and then detach the return springs (pliers work, alternatively a stout wire hook does the job). To avoid confusion, make a sketch of how the shoes came off so that they are replaced in the correction position.

You want to minimize brake fluid loss, so the flexible hose must be compressed. If you are careful, it can be squeezed closed using self-locking grips. But make sure that the jaws are covered with masking or insulating tape to avoid damaging the hose, and do not over-tighten the grips. A better bet is to use a purpose-made brake hose clamp, which uses parallel bars that exert even pressure and have no sharp edges to damage the rubber.

Now undo the hose from the cylinder half a turn. The metal brake pipe can be detached and then the two bolts which secure the cylinder to the back plate removed. Take out the bleed nipple and it can be pulled clear, then unscrewed from the flexible pipe union. If you're dealing with the other wheel cylinder, there is no need to detach the flexible hose, although it should still be clamped to avoid brake fluid loss.

Refitting a wheel cylinder is precisely the reverse of this procedure. Once on, the system must be bled and a bleeding tube on the nipple with the other end immersed in new fluid does the job in a few minutes, preferably with the aid of a helper to depress the brake pedal while you wait for the air bubbles to disappear.

Assessing wear of the brake shoes is straightforward. Basically, shoes should be replaced if the friction material is within 1/16th of an inch of the rivets or, with bonded linings, within 1/16th of an inch of the shoe itself. That is the absolute minimum, so if the limit is fast approaching make a mental note to fit new shoes in the near future.

If fluid contamination is slight the friction material can be cleaned with a proprietary solvent. Anything more than a surface film means replacement. Smear grease where the shoes mate with the cylinders and pivot points to guard against corrosion, but use the correct type because ordinary grease will melt. Your motor factor will supply you with HMP (high-melting point) grease whose specifications will include use on brakes. In any event, the whole assembly should be scrupulously clean and that necessitates removing dust. Don't blow it away because it can be harmful if inhaled. Use a soft brush instead.

If earlier you had difficulty removing the drum because of an internal ridge, the chances are that you will have similar difficulty refitting it. If the ridge is slight, you can overcome the problem by carefully relieving it with a hand-grinder. I'm

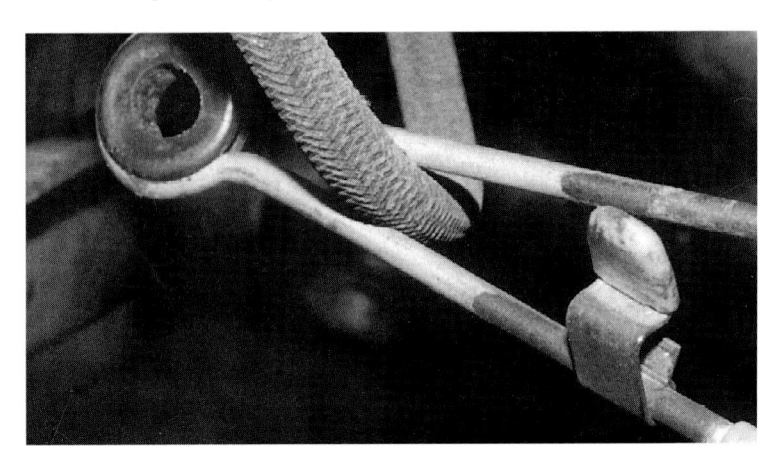

When working on wheel cylinders, the hose should be clamped to avoid fluid loss. Self-locking grips will do, but the pukka tool is far preferable.

With riveted brake shoes, replacement is necessary when the friction material has worn to within 1/16th of an inch of the rivets; that is the absolute minimum.

not suggesting you remove huge amounts of metal and really it's a case of using common-sense.

Brake adjustment is crucial with the front drum set-up; get it wrong and the system will work poorly and lead to excessive pedal travel. With the drum back in place, make sure that both adjusters are slackened off. The drum should spin completely freely without any hint of binding. Now turn one of the adjusters so that the drum locks solid. Slacken it gradually until the drum can be turned and lightly scuffs on the lining. Repeat the procedure for the other adjuster. Depress the brake pedal and then re-check the adjustments. You are aiming for a situation where both shoes are the same distance away from the drum, which will provide equal pressure and, thus, 100 per cent efficiency.

Earlier, I mentioned the dreaded Mini brake malady of a seized adjuster. It's square-headed and opens the shoes with a pin on a cam, and if it is mechanically simple it is also annoyingly prone to corrosion. Regular servicing, of course, helps prevent the adjuster clinging to the back plate, but even then it can easily fall foul of water and grime thrown up from the roads. If you are lucky, merely working the adjuster to and fro will remove corrosion and give you enough movement to set up the brakes. But really, that's just putting off a job until tomorrow that begs to be carried out today.

It's best to tackle the problem head-on to save yourself future grief because these adjusters can seize to the extent that the only answer is a new back plate. You'll need the shoes off to soak the offending adjuster with a releasing fluid – it may have to be left overnight and then more fluid applied. Now, gradually ease the adjuster to and fro until it operates freely. Smear it with HMP grease on either side of the back plate and wipe off the surplus.

I have to admit that I am still talking optimistically because even now, you may find that the adjuster refuses to budge to any degree. In this case you're faced with a straight choice, which is either to remove the back plate, immerse it in releasing fluid for a day or so and then grip the adjuster in a vice, or just bite the bullet and buy a

A popular Mini malady – seized brake adjusters. However, if they are given attention at every service, you should be able to avoid this problem.

new back plate. It's really a case of convenience and patience versus finances.

If you've replaced the linings on one side of your Mini, repeat the procedure on the other. They should always be replaced as sets to maintain even braking, also so that you know that the wear rate is even.

Hydraulic hoses – as tough and long-lived as they are – do need replacing now and again. Bend a hose in all directions and look for cracks or signs of perishing. The slightest imperfection means replacement. With the drum in place, get a friend to depress the brake pedal and watch and feel for ballooning of a hose. They can collapse internally and lose their ability to retain the massive hydraulic pressures imposed on them.

Disc brakes – as previously mentioned – are superior in just about all departments and are far less prone to fade than drums. The reason is that the discs expand with heat and therefore actually increase in size and make the pads press even tighter. On top of that, they rarely get excessively hot anyway because of the cooling effect of air flow

The minimum permissible thickness of friction material is 1/8th of an inch. You can check this visually without removing the pads, but they should come out at every major service regardless of your findings. Then you can clean and lubricate the mating surfaces on the pads and calipers.

Remove the split pins and retaining spring plate and each pad should come free using pliers. If not, use a stout screwdriver to push the pads (and, therefore, caliper pistons) away from the disc to provide a little clearance.

All mating faces should be smeared with HMP grease – don't forget the backs of the pads – to prevent seizure. If anti-rattle shims are fitted don't forget to refit them; they not only prevent the pads shaking around, but also stop squealing. In fact, their true noise-suppressing role should be pointed out, if only as a matter of interest and as a technical talking point.

Any mechanical component which is subject to friction will emit a noise. The shims do not stop the squealing, but actually change its frequency so that it is beyond the range of the human ear. This explains the somewhat odd situation when a dog (with its infinitely superior hearing range) will chase a car for no apparent reason.

Should you need to fit new brake pads the pistons will have to be pushed further back into the caliper to take into account the extra thickness of the friction material. Each piston can be eased inwards with a small tyre lever or stout screwdriver, but take care to push it back squarely. If it is retracted lopsidedly, it can damage a rubber seal. First, though, slacken the bleed nipple. This will allow displaced fluid to escape and avoid putting unwanted pressure on a seal, which could burst it. With the new pads in place and suitably greased, tighten the bleed nipple and then pump the pedal a few times. You will find that it will sink to the floor for the first couple of applications while the pads move out to meet the disc. Bleed the caliper and the job is done.

A leaking front caliper is a rarity – I've never come across one – but of course the seals can fail. Unlike with a wheel cylinder, a caliper is a fairly expensive item and fitting new seals is an option to be considered. Because of the physical size of the piston and its bore, it is quite easy to make a visual inspection for pitting or scoring. Anything less than a perfect surface means fitting a new caliper.

To strip this component, depress the pedal about halfway with the pads removed. This will make the pistons protrude slightly and facilitate removal. Loosen the flexible brake hose (first clamped to prevent fluid loss) and then unbolt the caliper. It can then be unscrewed from the hose and the pistons withdrawn for inspection. Clean it thoroughly and always lubricate with fresh brake fluid before reassembly to stop the seals tearing on dry metal.

One problem that disc brakes can suffer from is judder, which almost invariably is caused by disc run-out. A professional would check this with a dial gauge, but that's not the sort of equipment that the keen amateur is likely to have

– or ever need on a regular basis. However, you can check a disc for warping with nothing more sophisticated than a screwdriver.

Hold the blade to a fixed object – such as the side of the caliper – with the point on the disc face and rotate the disc. If there is run-out, it will be soon become apparent as the surface of the metal moves towards and away from the screwdriver blade. The permissible run-out is 10 thou or, perhaps more easily understood, about half the distance of a spark plug gap. If warping gives appreciably more movement you need a new disc.

All Minis have drum rear brakes and maintenance is exactly the same as with drums at the front except that there is just one adjuster per side. You do it up until the drum locks and then slacken it until the drum can be turned, scuffing lightly on the brake shoes.

The handbrake operates on the rear wheels, and although this can hardly be regarded as a vital safety item, it is something you will rely on in day-to-day driving and also put your trust in to help your Mini pass its MoT. With the brakes correctly adjusted, the handbrake should lock the wheels at the second click. Some testers will permit three clicks, but I would not lay a bet on it. If your handbrake doesn't hold on a steep incline the temptation is to adjust the cables (or cable on later models) from inside the car. After all, the adjusters are extremely easy to get at and appear to provide the ideal and most convenient solution. But that is not usually the case.

More commonly, a poor handbrake is caused by maladjusted brake shoes, so carry out this job first. If adjusting the shoes makes no difference, turn your attention to the quadrants, found on the top side of each radius arm. The quadrants are slotted and route the cables through right-angles from lever to the rear wheels. They are designed to pivot on pins, allowing the cables full movement, but seizure is a frequent occurrence, especially on high-mileage or neglected Minis. The trick is to soak them in penetrating fluid and repeat this process until they can pivot freely, aided by a few light taps with a small hammer.

A dial gauge will accurately measure run-out on a disc. However, as explained in the text, you can make a reasonable assessment using a screwdriver.

The job requires patience (which will be well rewarded), followed with generous greasing to prevent future problems.

If the handbrake still refuses to cope, it's now time to adjust the cable(s). With the earlier twin cables, adjust each a turn at a time with the rear jacked up and supported. The wheels should lock up at exactly the same moment. Operate the handbrake lever a few times and re-check the wheels to make sure none is binding with the lever in the 'off' position. This is most important to prevent overheating of the friction material. If you have run out of adjustment at the handbrake lever end, you know that the cables have stretched beyond their serviceable lives and need replacing.

I treat the master cylinder in exactly the same manner as wheel cylinders. That is, if it leaks then replace it. Experience has taught me that fitting new seals is something of a hit-and-miss affair and not to be chanced. Several types were fitted from the very basic, single-circuit component on earlier models to variations of the tandem-cylinder theme as the Mini came of age, the main difference being that the single-circuit cylinder feeds all four wheels with one piston whereas the tandem type has two pistons. Some versions use one piston to deal with the front and the other for the back, whereas others operate one front and one rear wheel on opposite sides with one circuit and the remaining two with the other.

As mentioned earlier, the rear wheels deal with a relatively small amount of braking and, therefore, the effort has to be lessened. With the earlier single-circuit master cylinder, this is achieved by a compensator valve on the rear subframe. If there is no fluid loss and the rear wheels do not lock up, the valve is in good order. However, if you trace fluid loss to this valve or the rear wheels lock – or if the brakes do not work on them at all – the valve must be replaced. Servicing it is not an option.

With the later tandem system, brake bias is dealt with by the master cylinder itself. However, some models still have a compensator valve (just examine the rear subframe) and, once again, it is not a serviceable item. Replacement is the answer.

Should you need to replace a metal brake pipe, tackle the job with a spanner which is a perfect fit on the union nut because they have the awful tendency to stick solid in their thread.

Working on relatively old pipework in the hydraulic system can be problematical, not the least of it being the tendency for threads to seize. It is important that the spanner is a precise fit on the union.

Pipe-flaring kits are available on a DIY basis but, as with a number of other tools, they are not something you will use that often and a motor factor will supply whatever pipe you need off the shelf. Alternatively, take the old pipe to a specialist motorists' shop to have a new one made up. Bend the new pipe so that it resembles the shape of the one you are replacing – but avoiding kinks or tight curves – and gently screw the unions into place, nipping them up. Now make the final adjustments to the pipe so that it does not chafe on any other component or rattle and finally tighten the unions. You can now bleed the system.

You have doubtless read many times how important it is to use new brake fluid – this advice crops up with monotonous regularity for the simple reason that it is absolutely vital. Hydraulic fluid is hygroscopic. In other words, it has the ability to absorb water. The amount of water it absorbs is dependent on time, therefore the older the fluid, the more water it will have taken in.

The boiling point of water is far lower than the temperature generated by brakes, so it does not take a scientific genius to work out that contaminated brake fluid can boil and you will be left with little more than steam to stop your Mini. An extreme scenario, agreed, but a most sobering thought. Quite apart from that, moisture can cause internal corrosion.

Even the experts are somewhat divided over how often brake fluid should be changed, but taking an average, the consensus is 36,000 miles or three years, whichever comes the sooner. I know plenty of professional mechanics who would not even bother to replenish the complete system, regardless of age or mileage, and work on the theory that it gets changed anyway through routine repairs and topping-up.

However, for the sake of the price of new fluid and, say, an hour's work, it is a job worth doing. It's basically a case of bleeding each wheel cylinder (or caliper) until new fluid comes through, topping up the master cylinder when appropriate. The bleeding sequence can vary,

The brake servo requires little attention. Periodically change the filter and check for leaks at the unions. Also, make sure that the pipe leading to the inlet manifold is in good condition because an air leak will cause rough running – which can be hard to pinpoint.

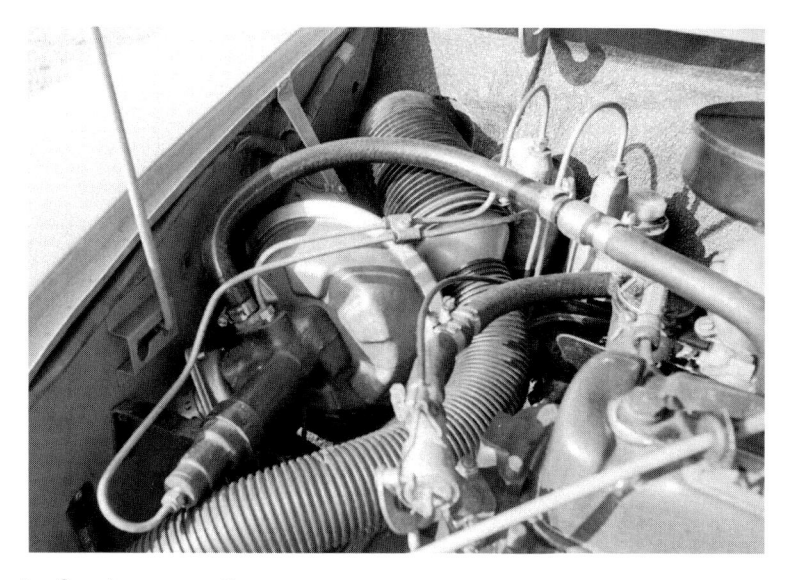

according to the type of master cylinder fitted, and you could tie yourself up in knots trying to identify exactly which type you have. But keep life simple and bleed the rear wheels first, then the fronts. This will always work, even though it might take a little longer than with the recommended sequence.

The Mini's brake lights are operated with an under-bonnet hydraulic switch on earlier models and an on-off electrical switch near the pedal on the later versions. The earlier switch cannot be repaired and if the brake lights fail to work (and there are no other electrical problems) the switch must be replaced.

The only other component on the braking system is the servo and it's what I would describe as a go, no-go item. It usually works or it doesn't, and although repair kits can be sourced I would always fit an exchange unit from a specialist.

The only attention it will require is the occasional change of air filter and inspection/replacement of the hose to inlet manifold. If this hose is at fault, not only will the servo be below par, but the engine will also idle roughly and be particularly 'lumpy' if the brake pedal is depressed at tickover. The quick way to check the operation of the servo is to depress the pedal to relieve the vacuum, then hold it down hard. Now start the engine and the pedal should sink. If it doesn't, the servo is at fault.

Suspension
The suspension set-up on the Mini is surprising for two reasons. The first is its sheer simplicity (apart from the Hydrolastic system, which will be dealt with a little later). It makes use of rubber cones instead of conventional coil or leaf springs, with basic, trailing radius arms at the rear and a shock absorber at each corner.

The second surprise is that, despite its relative crudeness, it works remarkably well, so well, in fact, that even in standard form the Mini has deservedly earned a reputation for incredible roadholding.

The Hydrolastic system – commonly referred to as 'wet' suspension – is relatively rare and unless you are going back to the Sixties, it's something you won't encounter. There is an hydraulic displacer unit at each corner and, in essence, when a front wheel goes up, the rear wheel goes down to compensate, and vice versa.

It's not known as a troublesome system, and provided there are no obvious leaks and the car sits evenly on the road you are almost guaranteed that all is well. If there is a leak or the car adopts a lopsided stance, it means either replacing an hydraulic pipe or displacer, depending on the symptom.

The system can be worked on only when it has been depressurized and that requires special equipment, as does repressurizing. This must be carried out by an appropriately equipped garage (unless you can obtain the equipment at a reasonable price, which is highly unlikely). The procedure would be to have the system depressurized, then carefully drive the car home, not exceeding 30mph. Then, a new displacer or hydraulic line can be fitted as appropriate and the car gingerly returned to the garage for the system to be pumped up.

Dealing with the rubber cone system – it's almost invariably referred to as 'dry' suspension – requires no special tools other than a spring compressor, which is a tool you cannot do without. Diagnosing a fault with dry suspension is, again, reasonably simple. Your Mini should sit evenly on the road and take corners and bumps without noticeable knocking, excessive body roll or one of the tyres touching the bodywork. A low ride height at one of the corners suggests that the rubber cone has either collapsed or perished.

Replacing a spring is not difficult, albeit a touch fiddly. It is best to remove the bonnet to improve access. Unbolt the plate on the appropriate side of the engine bulkhead crossmember and use your special tool to compress the spring. It screws into the middle of the rubber cone. Now, it is a case of jacking up and supporting the car in the usual way and removing the wheel. The suspension strut can be pulled free, followed by the cone, once the compressor has been unscrewed.

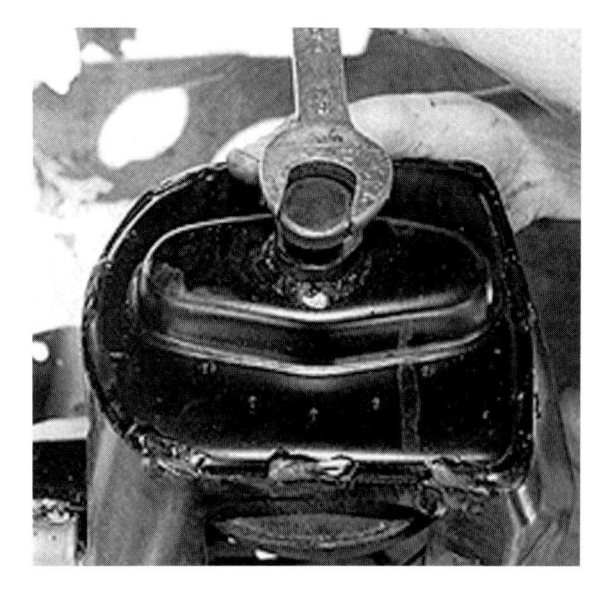

The rubber-cone suspension is removed and replaced using a pukka compressor.

Make sure the car is firmly supported whenever working on the suspension.

Like so many jobs on the Mini, it sounds complicated when expressed in words, but once you start wielding the spanners and removing the components in stages, you will find it almost self-explanatory. Examine the strut for corrosion because they can almost disintegrate over the years. Also, make a close check of the bottom knuckle joint and its cup and replace if there is serious pitting.

Checking shock absorbers requires observation and then a somewhat crude, but extremely effective, test. By observation, I mean exactly that. Examine the shock absorber for tell-

companies manufacturing shock absorbers.

In reality and from experience, I have found that life expectancy is more dependent on the type of use than the mileage. For example, you could easily dispose of a set of shocks in 30,000 miles with a hard-driven Mini used mainly on rough, country roads. Conversely, if the bulk of your driving is on decent A-roads and motorways then the lifespan could double at the very least. Rather than rely on mileage, I prefer to make an inspection and carry out the aforementioned bounce test.

Please bear in mind that shock absorbers have a significant effect on steering and roadholding because they not only control the rebound action of the suspension, but also, to a lesser extent,

The cups in which the suspension towers sit are prone to disintegration. Replace them if there is the slightest doubt.

The condition of the shock absorber bushes in important. However, the chances are that if they are worn the unit itself has reached the end of its useful life.

tale leaks; if there is seepage the unit is scrap.

The next move is to carry out the so-called bounce test. That is, bounce on each corner of the Mini until you have built up momentum and then release it. The car should come to rest after no more than one bounce. If it continues to oscillate and gradually comes to rest then you know that the shock absorber is due for replacement.

The subject of a shock absorber's useful lifespan is a trifle vexed. Some experts say that a unit will last for between 30,000 and 40,000 miles, although it has to be said, somewhat cynically, that most of those experts are

absorb shocks on compression. Maintaining near-perfect balance is important, therefore you should never replace one in isolation; always fit a new pair across each axle. Incidentally, if a shock absorber has been removed from your Mini it's advisable to leave it standing upright. The idea is that any air bubbles inside will travel to the top where they cannot cause any harm to the unit's action.

The Mini employs upper and lower suspension arms at the front which pivot on rubber bushes. Check them for obvious signs of perishing and follow that up by using a stout lever to waggle them from side to side. A small amount

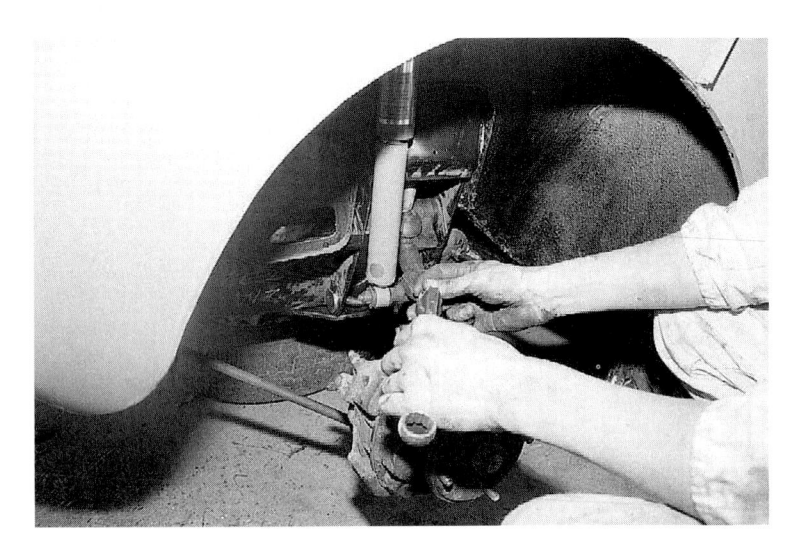

Whenever you are dealing with the swivels, it is best to remove the stub-axle assembly and take it to your bench.

You can check for play in the front suspension – that is, the swivel joints – using your hand and knee. A firm rocking motion will soon highlight excessive wear.

of free play is permissible.

If any of the bushes needs replacing, then quite obviously the relevant arm will have to come off the car. Because this is interlinked with splitting the swivel joints, this procedure is described later in the *steering* section.

The final check up front is on the rubber bump-stops, which are there to stop the suspension bottoming out. As with the rubber cones and bushes, they can perish after a long period and sometimes pull away from the metal plate to which they are bonded. If in doubt, replace them.

The rear suspension set-up also relies on rubber cones, but the up-and-down movement is dealt with by trailing arms, known as radius arms. Those of you who are familiar with older motorcycles will be well-versed in the principle, the difference being that on bikes, the set-up is referred to as a swinging arm and they are integral and move in unison.

On the Mini, each radius arm is attached to the subframe and can move independently, which not only benefits roadholding, but also enhances comfort (and even the staunchest of Mini fans would agree that anything which helps absorb the bumps is to be regarded as a bonus). Compared with the front end – which should not be too taxing to deal with, anyway – removing either of the rear rubber cones is even less complicated.

The procedure is exactly the same for either side except that when dealing with the nearside, the petrol tank will have to be removed. Undo the nut securing the top of the shock absorber, pull it clear and the radius arm will dangle free, with the car jacked up and supported and the wheel removed. If the damper body starts to turn while you are undoing the nut – which is quite likely – there is a flat on the shaft which will accept a spanner. With the radius arm hanging down, all you have to do is pull the strut and rubber cone free. The nylon cup which houses the knuckle should be inspected and replaced if damaged. You can prise it free with a screwdriver.

Replacement is a straight reversal, but be vigilant that the strut and spring are correctly located on their spigots and they do not slip out of place when the radius arm is raised to reconnect the shock absorber. You can check the radius arm bearings for wear by jacking up and supporting the car and vigorously pushing and pulling the wheel to feel for play. Obviously, the arm should go up and down, but not from side to side.

You will see that there is a grease nipple on the shaft, and if it is treated to a few strokes of the gun every 6000 miles, the bearings should last for absolutely ages. But unfortunately, it's not always a job which gets done and dry bearings quickly deteriorate. As an aside, they will creak and groan in a manner which is guaranteed to irritate.

With the car jacked and supported and the wheel removed, taking off the radius arm should present no problems. Remove the finishing plate on the outside (it's held with small set screws) and unscrew the outer and inner nuts on the shaft. Four bolts hold the outer bracket in place and with that removed, the radius arm can be pulled clear. Be careful not to lose the two thrust washers and the rubber seal which fits between the arm and side-member.

For whatever reason the radius arm has been removed, it would be sheer folly not to check the bearings and shaft. In fact, the condition of the shaft will tell you a great deal because if it is worn – and that will be patently evident by running your fingers along it to feel for grooves – it is an almost certain bet that the bushes will be worn, too.

Earlier Minis have bronze inner and outer bushes, while later models use a needle-roller bearing on the inner end. Removing bronze bushes can be exceedingly difficult and some enthusiasts have got away with chiselling them out (I'm one of them). But it's more than likely that you will damage the bore in the radius arm (I have also fallen into that category).

By far the best method is to buy or hire a suitable extractor or leave the job to a garage. Considering that the new bushes will have to be carefully pushed into place and then reamed out a fair degree, leaving the job to a fully-equipped mechanic makes sense. Having said that, if you are

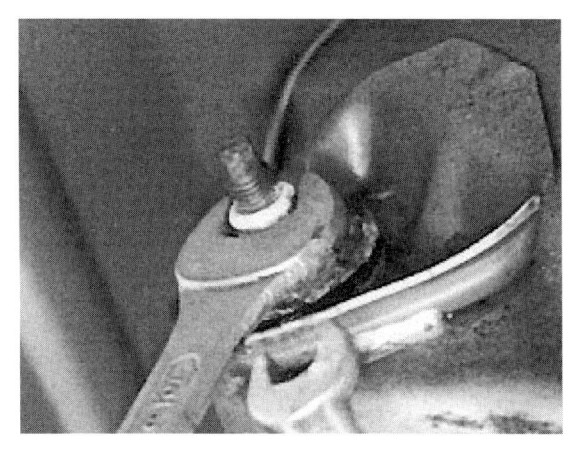

Use two spanners when undoing the top mounts on the rear shock absorbers; one spanner on the main nut and the other on the flats of the rod.

The long rod is the track-control arm and it keeps the wheel pointing in a straight line. Occasionally it can pull away from its mounting point on the body, in which case it will produce a violent pull to one side.

contemplating tackling the job on more than one occasion then, by all means, buy an extractor and reamer.

When dealing with a Mini with an inner needle-roller, this bearing, and the grease tube, should be removed before the outer bronze bush is reamed, otherwise they will become contaminated with swarf. Scrupulous cleanliness is important when reassembling, as is packing the components with grease.

It may seem a little out of sequence, at this juncture, to mention general maintenance of the suspension system, having spent some time describing repairs. That is because routine requirements are virtually nil. The most important job – as mentioned – is to treat the radius arm grease nipples to a few strokes of the gun every 6000 miles and inspect the shock absorbers for leaks. The rubber bushes on the front suspension arms can sometimes groan although they are not excessively worn. Coat them with a silicon spray every now and then. It will protect them and, hopefully, stop the noise.

Steering
A poor writer is often said to be guilty of repetition. If that is the case then I must stand accused, because I feel compelled to repeat what has been said several times elsewhere, namely that some aspects of the Mini amaze me with both their crudeness and their effectiveness.

Fitting perfectly into both categories is the knuckle – or swivel – joint set-up for the front wheels. Nowadays, when grease guns have virtually been relegated to the history books and sealed-for-life swivels are totally taken for granted, the Mini stands almost alone in employing knuckle joints which not only require fairly frequent attention, but are also serviceable items. In essence, the system is just one technological step ahead of the old-fashioned kingpin arrangement, which was also serviceable, but more troublesome to repair.

Dealing with the swivels is one of the most common steering jobs you will carry out because they are a popular – used in its purest sense –

MoT failure point, either because there is excessive play or because they are binding.

On a preventive note, each joint should receive a few strokes of the grease gun every 6000 miles. Pump in the grease until it starts to appear from the top of the dome nut; you then know that ample lubricant has reached the working parts. As a bonus, packing in the grease will take care of small amounts of free play. But I do mean small – just a few thousandths of an inch.

Diagnosing play in a swivel takes only a few minutes. Jack up and support the car, then grasp the wheel with hands at the six o'clock position. Waggle it firmly and feel for movement. Ideally, there should be none, although the tiniest amount is permissible for the MoT.

Experience will tell you if a knuckle is worn. If you're still in doubt, pull and push the wheel using one hand and your knee. Put your other hand over the upper swivel so that you can feel the suspension arm and the stub-axle (which carries the disc or drum assembly). You want to be able to feel both components at the same time to see if the stub-axle moves in relation to the suspension arm. Then repeat the exercise for the lower swivel. When a swivel joint wears on a Mini, it usually does so in grand fashion and play will be all too apparent.

On a safety note, make absolutely sure that the car is firmly supported on an axle stand and be careful that the wheel is not turned laterally, trapping your fingers.

Diagnosing a binding swivel is not so easy. Having said that, it's also relatively rare, unless the joint has been starved of grease or it was never correctly shimmed in the first place. Tell-tale symptoms are heavier-than-normal steering and the tendency for your Mini to stay on a chosen course when leaving a corner, losing its ability to self-centre and then steer in a straight line. If the steering feels normal and behaves as it should, the odds are highly in favour of the swivels having free movement.

I recall many years (and many Minis) ago when my Cooper S failed on a tight swivel. The garage quoted what to me was an extortionate sum for putting matters right, so doing the job myself seemed the pertinent course of action. It took me ages, but eventually I emerged victorious from what I perceived as a major mechanical victory. Yet with hindsight and experience, it's a job I now regard as little more than routine. You will soon feel the same.

If you have established that a swivel is either too slack or binding, attention is obviously required. First, you have to disconnect the track-rod end from the steering arm (with the wheel off and the car supported) and then a workshop manual will tell you that the split-pin has to come out, using a pair of pliers – a beautiful thought in an ideal world. But as we all know, the world is rarely ideal, and unless you are lucky, the split-pin will have rusted into its hole.

If you can't push it through with a fine punch, slightly more brutal action is required. Undo and remove the castellated nut so that it shears through the pin. With improved access, a fine punch should knock it through, and by a fine punch, I do not preclude a small nail. It may not seem exactly high-tech as a solution, but it almost always works. But if that fails, a tiny drill will do the job, though using a drill this small requires a degree of care because they break amazingly easily.

The track-rod end comes free using a ball-joint splitter. The wedge type will do, but it's prone to ripping the rubber gaiter, and therefore the screw type is preferable *(this was dealt with in the chapter on equipping your workshop)*. If you possess neither, you should be able to shock the taper free by striking each side of the eye with hammers used in unison.

If you don't mind having a mechanical wrestling match on your hands, it is possible to work on the swivels with the hub *in situ*, but take my word, it is far, far preferable to remove the assembly and carry out the work on your bench. I will assume that you have chosen the second option.

Remove the hub-retaining nut and then the brake line. Each swivel is held with a tapered shank – much the same as the track-rod end – and a splitter will separate them. The hammer shock treatment is effective, but it can be time-consuming. The assembly comes free by levering the bottom suspension arm downwards.

You can buy a large socket or ring spanner to undo the domed nuts, but an adjustable wrench works just as well, especially when you're on the bench with the vastly-improved access you will now be afforded.

At this juncture you may hark back to my earlier comments about crudeness because there is nothing more inside than a knuckle joint which sits in a cup and a selection of shims, other than the bottom swivel, which has a small spring.

You may recall that in the earlier section of this chapter covering *brakes* I wrote about dealing with faulty master and wheel cylinders. The advice then was to fit new and not bother with repairs, on the basis that weighing up economy against the chances of success, brand new components are nearly always a clear winner. Put far more simply, a swivel joint kit is so cheap that it makes no sense at all to use part-worn components.

Now you can have a little fun in discovering the somewhat hit-and-miss nature of correctly assembling the Mini's swivels. In theory, arriving at the optimum adjustment – that is, free movement without too much play or the tendency to bind – is a scientific exercise, but in practice it requires experimenting with shims (a

The split-pin on a castellated nut is removed using pliers. It's always preferable to fit a new item.

The text explains how to decide which shims to fit to achieve smooth operation of the swivels. The arrows indicate where you should take measurements with feeler blades. The top swivel is on the left, alongside the lower swivel (which is spring-loaded).

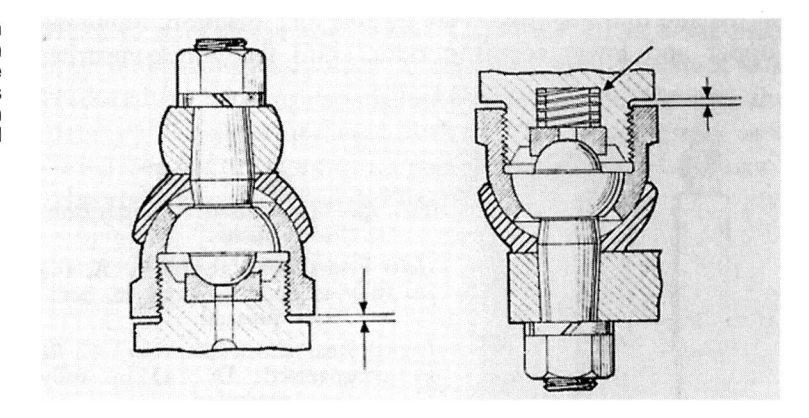

selection is provided with each swivel joint kit).

I would now love to tell you how I have adjusted countless swivel joints with a minimum of fuss and achieved total perfection. But I like to tell the truth, and I have to admit I have never got the job right at the first attempt. But as a form of consolation, I have managed to refine the task from being haphazard to relatively precise.

First, I want you to consider the official workshop procedure, even though I have found this to be definitely subject to aberrations. Remember that the lockwasher, give or take a few thousandths of an inch, is some 35 thou thick. Now screw the swivel into place, without the lockwasher (and the spring, in the case of the lower swivel) until it cannot move, but do not over-tighten it. A firm hand pressure or a slight nip with your spanner will do it.

Now measure the gap between the bottom of the dome nut and the ball-joint seat. Subtract 35 thou (the thickness of the lockwasher) and fit shims to that thickness. So, for example, if the gap is 80 thou, you need shims to the equivalent of 45 thou. Reassemble the swivel with the appropriate shims and lockwasher and adjustment should be perfect.

All fine and well, except for one snag – deciding which shims add up to 45 thou. Without a micrometer (a tool you will be unlikely to have, let alone need on a regular basis), this is extremely difficult. Therefore, better to do it this way. Assemble the swivel joint as described, then push shims into the gap until they form a snug fit, and that is a matter of trial and error. It's what some refer to as a 'go, no-go situation'. You keep adding shims until they no longer fit and then remove them, one by one and thinnest first, until they slide into place.

Hopefully, you have now arrived at the correct shims, and if you get the required adjustment with the shims and lockwasher in place and the dome nut fully tightened (and the assembly packed with grease) then well done. If not, you will have joined the many thousands of owners who have spent 30 minutes or so chopping and changing shims for the desired result.

So how do you know when a swivel is correctly adjusted, the point being that it is a matter of judgment and not, as with adjusting the tappets or the ignition timing, something which can be finitely measured? Well, imagine you have plunged a knife into cold butter and you are moving it from side to side. The resistance is firm, but not overly obstructive. That is exactly what you should feel when moving the swivel shank from side to side. The whole assembly is ready to go back on your Mini, the finishing touch being the grease gun treatment until grease shows from the top of the dome nut.

Grease nipples, for all their simplicity, can cause trouble, usually by clogging with age, in which case they will not allow grease to pass through. Insert the nipple into your gun and then pump it until grease appears. If it won't, then soak the nipple in solvent (cellulose thinners, for example) to clean it; and if that fails to work, fit a new nipple.

Another common job you will encounter is replacing a worn track-rod end. Checking for wear means jacking up and supporting the car and waggling the wheel with hands at the quarter-to-three position to feel for play. But do not confuse it with wear in the steering rack. If you are in doubt, get a friend to push and pull on the wheel and use your hand to feel for play in the track-rod end.

A further test you can carry out to help you distinguish between a worn track-rod end and wear in the rack is to turn the steering wheel one way and then the other, when each road wheel should respond immediately without slop. The MoT test allows half an inch of movement at the steering wheel rim before the road wheels move. If play is greater then you know that the rack is at fault. Dealing with a faulty rack is covered a little later.

Track-rod ends are not serviceable items so wear means replacement. They are secured with locknuts and, once the taper has been split, simply unscrew from the rods. It is important that a track-rod end is replaced in the same position, so slacken the locknut (using a spanner on the flat of the rod to stop it turning) the minimum amount.

It is advisable – although not always necessary – to have the toe-in checked at a garage after fitting a new track-rod end because if it is incorrect, you will get steering bias and uneven tyre wear.

When fitting a new track-rod end or, indeed, refitting the existing one, it's highly likely that the taper will turn in its eye, which means you cannot tighten the nut. Overcome this by placing a jack underneath the swivel and applying moderate pressure. This will lock the taper in place and allow the nut to be screwed up.

Dealing with worn rubber bushes in the upper and lower suspension arms is by no means technically difficult. It is merely a case of removing the pivot bolt and then pulling the arm clear. The bushes should simply pull out. With the lower suspension arm, you do have the added hassle of the tension from the tie rod, but that can be overcome with judicial use of a stout screwdriver as a lever. When fitting new bushes, smear them with silicone grease to aid fitting and to protect them from perishing.

Talk to the uninitiated and they will tell horrific tales about replacing a Mini steering rack. However, the initiated will tell you that you need nothing more than a few simple tools and the ability to plough on when patience is wearing a little thin.

Before dismissing your rack as in need of replacement, make a couple of checks. The first is on the base of the steering column where it is held to the splined shaft of the rack with a bolt

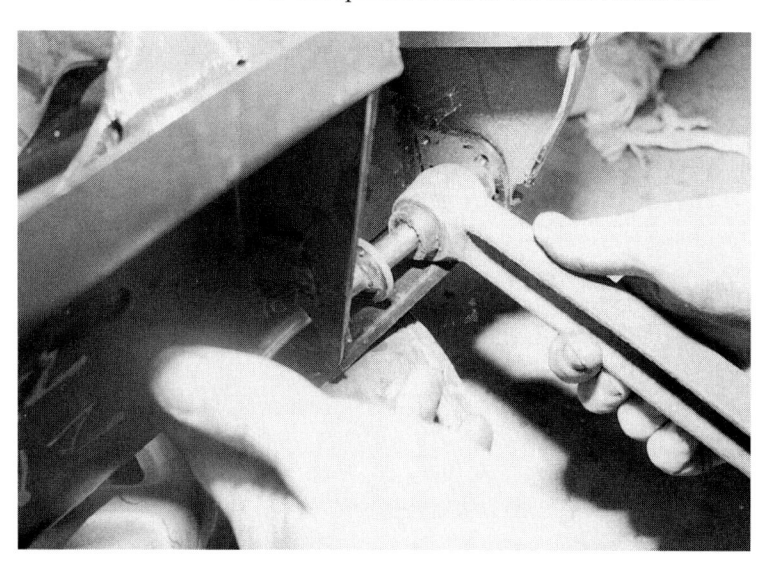

The suspension arms are held to the body with long bolts, which often seize. Soak them in penetrating fluid.

Removing and replacing bushes on the suspension arms is best done on the bench, using a suitable tube (such as a socket) to push them out.

and locknut. Make sure that they are firmly tightened. However, do not overdo matters because the collar on the column is merely mild steel and can be squashed out of shape, which could eventually lead to it splitting with a resultant loss of steering.

The other check is on the security of the nuts on the U-clamps which hold the rack in place. Lift the carpets and you will see them. If they work loose, there will be play in the steering, and quite often it manifests itself as a small, but definite click when you change direction.

A steering rack is also prone to binding, which is checked by jacking up and supporting the car and turning the steering wheel from one lock to the other. Tight spots will be easy to detect.

Now for steering rack replacement. As you will recall in the introductory piece, a workshop manual is an essential part of your toolkit and you should first have studied rack removal in detail. This is by no means an attempt by the author to casually gloss over the procedure, but I see little point in presenting you again with a blow-by-blow, nut-by-nut account of what is involved. The fact is that the job may sound immensely difficult when put down on paper, but in reality it means being methodical, then everything will become apparent as you progress.

In essence, you need to separate the steering column from the rack, which means undoing the bottom pinch bolt and then the bolt which holds the middle of the column housing to the parcel shelf. You may find it has a shear bolt, in which case, shear it off and cut a groove in it so that a screwdriver can be used.

Jack up and support the car and remove the road wheels. The shock absorbers are disconnected at their lower ends, the track-rod ends removed, exhaust mounting bracket taken off, engine stabilizer bar (from engine to bulkhead) removed and the clutch master cylinder removed so that it hangs free.

Now support the body of the car, using strategically placed pieces of stout wood under the front wheelarches, and support the rear of the subframe with jacks. The subframe has to be lowered by about 1½ inches to give clearance for the rack's U-clamps to be taken off so, in effect, you are removing all components which would stop it coming down.

Unbolt the rear of the subframe and then lower it. You may find that it needs to be levered down the final few inches. The U-clamps can be pulled clear and, with a fair amount of juggling, the rack will come out on the driver's side. An experienced Mini mechanic will do the job in about three hours, so allow yourself five to be on the safe side.

Market forces – and pure convenience – dictate that new (or reconditioned) racks come complete, that is, sealed and with new gaiters fitted. Be grateful for that because servicing a rack is a job for a professional and you should fit new gaiters as a matter of course.

One extremely important point is to refit the track-rod ends in the same position as they were removed, so measure the distance from the locknuts to the end of the rods. If, for example, one track-rod end is screwed in an extra half an inch, the other one will have to be fitted half an inch further out to compensate and get the wheels aligned. That means that even though you could get the toe-in perfectly adjusted by a garage, the steering will always be off-centre, which would mean you would get more steering lock one way than the other. Hardly a disaster, but annoyingly inconvenient.

When the rack has been refitted, set the wheels in the straight-ahead position and then reconnect the steering column to the rack so that the steering wheel is in its normal position, with the spokes at the ten-to-two position. Check that the left- and right-hand locks have an equal number of turns. If you have positioned the track-rod ends correctly and the steering lock is equal on both turns, all you need to do is to have the tracking adjusted.

Of course, life can be kinder and all you could be faced with is replacing a split steering rack gaiter. Early models have black gaiters, which are filled with oil, while later Minis have transparent gaiters, which take grease. A split gaiter is an MoT failure, not to mention a threat to the well-being of the rack-and-pinion mechanism because an ingress of dirt and water will wreak havoc.

The gaiter comes off once the track-rod end has been removed and the securing wire or clips taken off. Slide the new gaiter into place and fill with oil, using a can, or grease (grease gun) as appropriate and then turn the steering wheel from side to side to work in the lubricant.

On a far cleaner and more mechanically sociable note, the only other job you are likely to encounter is replacing the nylon bush at the top of the steering column or the felt bush at the bottom. Again, excess movement means an MoT failure, although testers vary wildly on what they judge to be excess.

Remove the plastic housings and then the indicator stalk assembly. Remove the steering wheel, the steering column from the rack and then the parcel shelf and pull it clear. The top bush can be prised free with a screwdriver and then the bottom bush simply slides off. It's as easy as that.

CHAPTER 8

The fuel system

Fault-finding and carburettor tuning

THE MINI'S fuel system is just about as outdated as you can get, compared with modern machinery. But by no means take that as a negative because for outdated, I want you to read simple. And simplicity, as is almost always the case, equates to ease of maintenance and fault diagnosis. It is unquestionable that the latest systems on cars – governed either by an electrical control unit, computer or both – are incredibly reliable. They are also totally beyond the home enthusiast – unless exceedingly well-endowed with both knowledge and equipment – to diagnose or repair.

But the Mini has a humble set-up of pump and SU carburettor, with a few other pieces of paraphernalia. Even the twin SUs on Cooper variants will give you no horrors, with a logical and patient approach.

You will notice that fuel injection has so far not been mentioned and there are good reasons. For a start – and this is admittedly personal – I have never associated the Mini with anything other than carburettors because, to me, they represent the pure essence of the vehicle. And that is traditional simplicity.

Secondly, although there are certain jobs you can carry out on a Mini's injection system, it is by and large dependent on an ECU and, therefore, specialist. You could spend fruitless hours trying to pinpoint a fault whereas a specialist will plug into the diagnostic socket and get an immediate read-out. Quite apart from that, tinkering with the system's associated components can damage the ECU. In short, I wouldn't mess around with it other than to change filters, check for leaks and ensure that all of the electrical connections are secure and clean.

As a matter of interest, many assume that fuel injection is used (not only on the Mini) as a performance-enhancer. Well, that is not the case. Injection does provide slightly crisper throttle response compared with carburettors, but its main advantage is its ability to run super-efficiently and, therefore, produce the minimum emissions (in today's world, a high-profile issue).

If you want the ultimate performance, nothing – except, perhaps, a bucket – can deliver fuel in such copious quantities as a carburettor. If you doubt that, ask yourself why instruments such as the enormous Weber 48DCOE carbs are still immensely popular.

But back to home, and humbler ground. Let's look at the SU. Take one apart and you will quickly see that the main components are the piston, dashpot, jet needle and jet, float chamber and needle valve to allow fuel in, but prevent flooding.

Push down on the throttle and the depression in the inlet manifold causes the piston to rise in its dashpot, lifting the jet needle and

The old and the new – one of the earliest SU carburettors alongside a modern version.

increasing fuel flow and air at the same time. No need for an accelerator pump and virtually no chance of the jet becoming blocked, purely because of its size. Wonderfully simple (ask millions of Morris Minor, MG Midget, MGB, XK and early XJ Jaguar owners).

The only routine maintenance requirement is occasionally topping up the dashpot with light oil. With high-mileage Minis, use a slightly heavier oil (a normal multigrade, for example) to overcome wear. That will prevent the piston flying up in the dashpot too quickly under sudden acceleration and possibly causing slight hesitation.

Actually defining, mileage-wise, when an SU requires attention or replacement is not a scientific exercise because it is heavily dependent on the type of driving. Obviously enough, if your Mini spends most of its time in traffic, the carburettor will be working a lot harder than in a car used for long runs when less use is made of the throttle. Having said that, the SU should last for at least 80,000 miles before you experience any problems as a result of wear.

So what are the potential problems? Well, the most common is an incorrect mixture. Sooty plugs mean it's too rich, while plugs with whitish deposits mean it is running too lean. As a back-up to your diagnosis, a rich mixture will result in an engine which chugs, will usually start from cold without choke, but be reluctant to fire up when hot. However, check first that the air filter element is not dirty. A lean mixture will often lead to an engine running a little on the hot side and with a marked hesitance – that is, a flat spot – when accelerating suddenly.

On most carburettors, the mixture is adjusted with an air control screw, usually on the side of the body, but the SU is different. You set the mixture by turning the large adjuster nut at the base of the carb. Unscrewing it lowers the jet and richens the mixture. Screw it up and it gets leaner. Pukka spanners are available to adjust the jet. They are thin and angled to provide good access. However, if you've got a grinder handy, you can trim down a conventional spanner and cut off part of the shank.

Unless the mixture is way out, half a turn in either direction should achieve what you are after. Basically, you should unscrew it to richen the mixture until the engine stumbles. Now do it up until the same thing happens. A setting just about midway should provide the perfect mixture. If the adjustment procedure takes more than a few minutes, you will need to rev the engine hard to purge the carb, otherwise there will be a slight build-up of fuel, which will give you a false reading.

Most SUs have a small metal lifting pin at their base, which allows you to further check the setting. Push it up progressively and listen to the engine note. The revs should rise slightly and then settle back to an even speed. If there is a noticeable increase in revs, which does not die down, the mixture is too weak. Conversely, should the engine begin to chug, you will know that the mixture is too rich.

Setting the mixture on an SU requires a bit of practice, but you will quickly fall into the routine. You can, of course, use a CO meter on the exhaust, which will give you a scientific reading. However, I prefer to use judgment because a meter will give you recommended limits (usually as lean as possible), whereas an engine will run healthier if set slightly – and I *mean* slightly – too rich.

The reason is that although the internal combustion process obviously requires fuel/air to be burnt as efficiently as possible, it is also essential that a small proportion of unburnt fuel – hydrocarbons – passes through the engine. They provide vital cooling for the upper cylinder.

Once satisfied that the mixture is correct, take your Mini for a run to see whether the engine responds under acceleration. Now check the plugs. Ideally, their tips should be a lightish brown. If one plug in isolation has white deposits (weak mixture) there is every chance that the inlet manifold is leaking on that cylinder.

All attempts at adjusting the mixture could fail. In that case, the manifold gasket has probably blown in more than one place or the gasket between the carb and manifold is leaking. Alternatively, the carburettor face which mates to the manifold could be warped. Check it with a straight edge and, if there is a discrepancy, dress up the aluminium using a sheet of glass and 800-grit wet-or-dry abrasive paper to restore the surface.

One other fault which can drastically affect the mixture is a leak in the brake servo hose which connects to the manifold. Check for this by removing the hose and blocking off the stub. If the engine runs correctly you have pinpointed the fault. A quick diagnosis of the inlet joints can be made with maintenance spray. Run the engine and squirt each joint to see if the fluid is sucked away.

Another important check on the SU is to make sure that the piston rises and falls freely. Remove the piston damper and then the air cleaner assembly and insert your finger into the mouth of the carburettor (engine stopped, of course). Lift the piston and let it fall. It should drop immediately.

If it doesn't then there are three possible causes. The first, and most likely, is that the jet is not central with the needle. Undo by about a turn and a half the large nut which holds the jet at the base of the carb (it's above the mixture nut), then use your finger to push the piston up. Let it fall and repeat the exercise. This should

The SU is a pretty basic – although efficient – instrument. The dashpot comes off to reveal the piston. Keep the piston and bore clean for smooth action, but use nothing more than paraffin and wire wool.

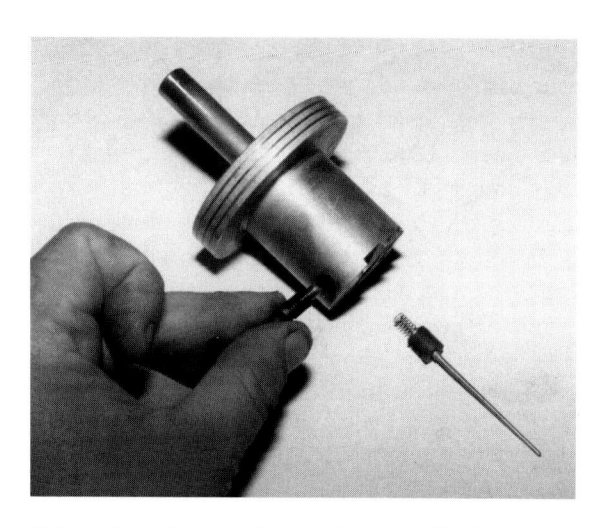

If the piston refuses to rise and fall smoothly, the jet may need centralizing (see text). However, it could be a bent needle; remove it and check against a straight edge.

centralize the jet and the holder can be retightened.

If this fails to free the piston, suspect a bent needle. Take off the dashpot cover and hold the needle against a straight edge, such as a steel rule. The only other cause of a restriction is a dirty or scored piston. It can be lightly cleaned using steel wool and paraffin. But, bearing in mind that it is a reasonably precise fit in its bore, only the lightest of abrasion is permissible.

If your carburettor floods, check the needle valve which rests on the float in the float chamber. Blow through it to clear dirt and make sure it is not sticking. With the old-type, brass float, shake it to see if petrol has got inside, signifying a leak. You can often seal this with careful use of solder. The later plastic type is much tougher and not prone to problems.

You might find that it is impossible to obtain an even tickover, even though the mixture is spot-on. A most irritating situation when the idle speed is just about right and then, after a couple of depressions of the throttle, it either slows down and the engine dies or it speeds up. Check that the throttle return spring is connected and still has plenty of tension. If the spring is serviceable the butterfly spindle and/or its bearings are almost certainly worn. This allows the spindle to move sideways and jam.

It is possible to buy service kits for SU carbs – typically with a new needle, jets and needle valve. Well, when this carburettor is fairly worn, replacing parts piecemeal is not a good idea. Just buy a new carburettor – they are reasonably priced and readily available. Then the job is done completely.

Incidentally, it is tempting to remove the butterfly and spindle from the carburettor for cleaning because, it could be argued, a clean carb is a better carb. However, over the years the small build-up of carbon and gummy deposits actually compensates for wear. So leave well enough alone.

The idea of tuning twin carburettors has struck something tantamount to abject fear in the hearts of many home enthusiasts. But really it is not that difficult and requires little more than patience and a good ear. Here is the procedure: First, slacken the throttle linkage so that each carburettor can operate independently of the other. Get the engine warm and ticking over at its correct speed (about 850rpm). Now slacken off one of the throttle-stop screws so that one of the carburettors is taken out of action and the engine is running on the other.

Set the mixture as described earlier, take the carb out of commission with the tickover screw and repeat the procedure for the other instrument. They are both tuned as far as mixture goes. It's now a case of getting them synchronized. Having both carburettors open at precisely the same moment is vital if you are to enjoy clean and satisfying acceleration without flat-spots.

Run the engine and carefully adjust both idle screws so that the tickover is as even as you can achieve. With the air filters removed, use a tube to listen to the hiss from each intake (special listening tubes are available). Each hiss should be the same. That sounds almost ludicrous on paper, I agree, but once you have tried it, you will soon realize how easy it is to distinguish between the different tones of intake noise.

Adjust the tickover screws so that each hiss is identical. Now adjust the screws again – each by the same amount – so that the tickover is even and at the desired speed. So now the mixtures are correct and the carburettors are in synchronization at tickover. The final step is to make sure that they continue to open in unison and this is achieved by adjusting the throttle linkage between the carburettors. This adjustment is set at the factory and rarely goes wrong. Nevertheless, observe the action very closely.

There is one final check and it's a tip I picked up years ago and one of my favourite non-workshop manual procedures. With the air cleaners removed, place two identical small objects in the intakes of each carburettor under each piston cutaway (small spoons, for example, are fine). Gradually increase the revs and watch your spoons, or whatever. They will tip downwards as the pistons rise. Do they fall in exact unison? An amazingly accurate means of checking synchronization.

Naturally, the market for special tools has moved with demand, and over the years a number of devices have been developed for balancing twin carburettors. Some rely on air depression, some rely on a head of liquid, visible in a tube (similar visually to a giant thermometer). I have so far never found the need to resort to any such thing, but feel free because many owners have found them invaluable.

Fairly precise procedures are laid down for adjusting the choke mechanism, involving taking measurements with feeler blades. In reality, life is much simpler. All you need do is adjust the cable so that there is at least a quarter of an inch of free movement of the choke knob and a small gap – about an eighth of an inch – between the choke cam (on the side of the carb) and its attendant screw on the throttle mechanism. In other words, you want a little slack in the choke cable and to adjust the screw so that the choke knob has to be pulled out about a third of the way before it starts operating the throttle.

The idea is that when starting from cold you cannot over-rev the engine using the choke, which would cause havoc with the big-end and main bearings before the oil has had a chance to circulate.

You will gather from other parts of this book that I am generally full of praise for the Mini's overall design. But the Mini – like the world – is not without its faults and the positioning of the electric SU fuel pump on earlier models ranks high on the list of failings. After all, I cannot think of a more vulnerable location to affix it. Living on the underside, attached to the subframe, the pump is subjected to the worst abuses imaginable of the elements. The fact that it survives so well is a matter of wonder to me.

The actual thinking behind its location is obviously that space is saved inside the boot or under the bonnet. A cue could have been taken from the designers of the Mark 2 Jaguar, who

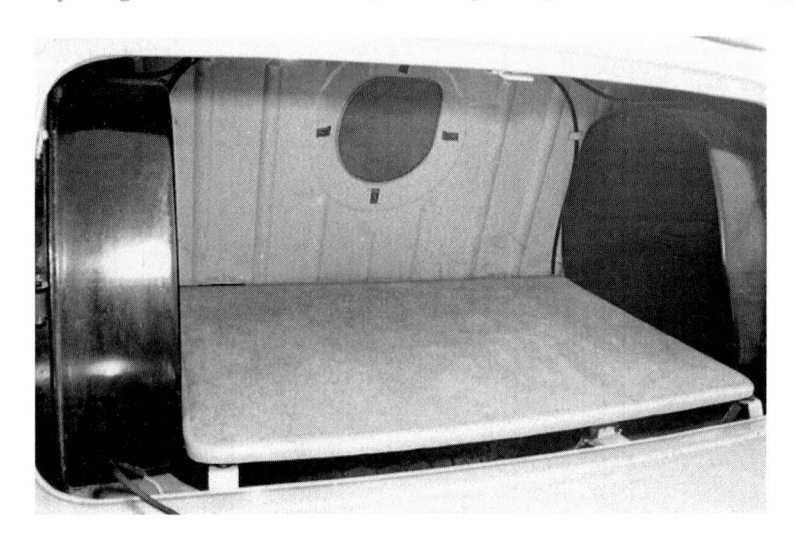

The fuel tank is easily accessible, in fact it is probably easier to get at than on almost any other car. It can be cleaned internally, as explained in the text. The car pictured is a Cooper S with optional twin tanks.

preferred to sacrifice space and give the pumps protection, because on that car they are far more sensibly mounted inside the boot. And indeed, most Coopers converted for rallying had their pumps moved inside by sensible owners.

My feelings aside, the pumps are on the underside and you will have to live with that, unless you fancy a conversion job, as per the rally cars. At every major service, treat the pump to liberal doses of maintenance spray and check the connections. It is possible to fit new points to an SU electric pump should it fail, but fitting a new pump is far more advisable. Accessing the pump is so inconvenient that you really do not want to do the job more frequently than necessary.

On later Minis, a mechanical pump was fitted on the side of the block, operated from the camshaft. Just as efficient and out of harm's way. With either type of pump, fault diagnosis is simple enough. If the car fails to start or breaks down and you suspect the pump, disconnect the fuel line at the carburettor and make sure it is pointing out of harm's way – that is, away from a hot exhaust manifold. Just switch on the ignition to check delivery of an electric pump. The engine should be turned on the starter to test the action of a mechanical pump.

In either case, fuel should flow copiously. As a roadside emergency measure, tapping an electric pump will sometimes spur it into life. Use a rubber mallet and go carefully, otherwise you will smash through the casing. An inoperative mechanical pump should be replaced.

Should you experience starting problems or your Mini judders to a halt and you have established that the pump is working, suspect the needle valve in the float chamber. Remove the cover and see if there is petrol inside. If not, the needle valve is blocked.

Apart from the carburettor and pump, the only other component in the fuel system is, of course, the tank, and it must be said that with extremely few exceptions, no other car offers such easy access to this item. It's in the boot and held with a strap.

The chances are that you will never need to remove it. However, in the unlikely event that the inside should become contaminated – such as with corrosion – then, provided it is not severe, you should be able to cure the problem. Remove the tank, block the outlet stub and pour shingle inside, followed by about a quarter of a gallon of petrol. Shake the tank vigorously for a few minutes – the help of a friend makes life easier – then pour away the shingle and petrol. The abrasive action should clear any scaling or surface corrosion.

Follow up by flushing the tank through with boiling water. Water? In a petrol tank? Well, it will clean the inside and, as long as it is straight out of a kettle and not just luke-warm, any excess will quickly evaporate. In any event, it will pay you to keep your tank topped up as much as possible during normal running so that the interior surface is covered with petrol rather than being exposed to oxygen.

CHAPTER 9

The bodywork

Panel repairs, replacement and paint spraying

BODYWORK damage – either through corrosion or from an accident – has written off, and will probably continue to write off, more cars than any other single factor. The reasons are twofold. Firstly, having it repaired is exceedingly expensive and, therefore, it takes relatively little body damage to make a car beyond economical salvation. Secondly, many owners fight shy of tackling jobs themselves and, whereas they would happily embark on a complete mechanical overhaul, the prospect of dealing with damaged panels is treated almost as a taboo subject.

This is understandable because whereas there are many mechanics around who are happy to share their knowledge, professional panel beaters and sprayers are fewer and farther between and they seem somewhat reluctant to share their skills. To compound matters, if you are really going to get into body repairs you do need specialized equipment which, compared with what's required for mechanical work, is relatively expensive. Notice that I said relatively because, as mentioned in the chapter on *equipping your workshop*, the price of many tools, such as compressors and welders, is now remarkably reasonable. It's really a case of you deciding which level you want to attain.

Dealing with dents
I was incredibly fortunate in knowing a professional bodywork man for a number of years and he taught me a great deal. Perhaps the most significant thing I learned was that there is no magic involved in repairing metalwork. It does have something of a glamorous image. You take a car into a body shop with a nasty dent and several days later it emerges from the workshop as if nothing had ever happened. But take it from me, restoring contours and then applying paint is purely a matter of patience and, to a great degree, precise use of your equipment.

Before considering the more advanced jobs – including a complete respray – let's first consider the most frequent problems and how to deal with them. If you are tackling a dent, the first job is to minimize the damage as much as possible. If you can gain rear access so much the better. You will not need special dollies, just a ball-pein hammer and its larger brother (a club hammer is ideal). Tap the centre of the dent from the inside while holding the heavier hammer on the outside where the metal has creased. By this method, you will gradually knock out the dent, but prevent the metal from distorting. The idea is to remove as much of the dent as possible while leaving the metal slightly concave to accept filler.

This method works well with what I would term a sharp dent – the result of a direct impact. However, you might be faced with a long, gentle crease in a door panel. You will quite often find that the metal will spring back into a reasonable shape by using a rubber mallet.

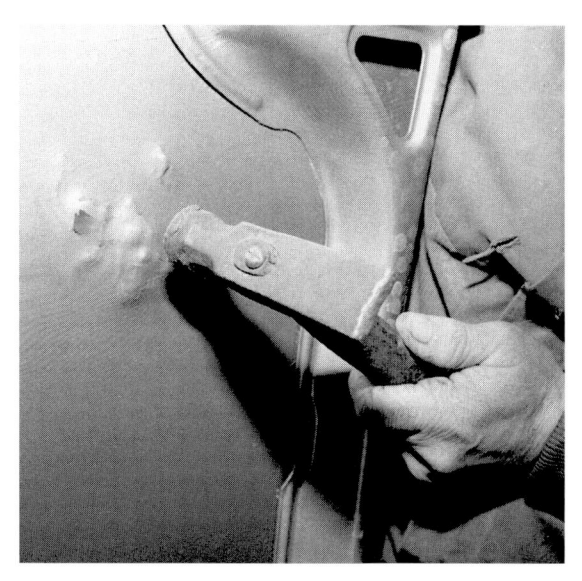

As an alternative, large and powerful rubber suckers are available which are attached to panels and then pulled out sharply. A cheaper, but more brutal, method is to drill a hole in the middle of the dent and insert a self-tapping screw. You can pull on that using self-locking grips. A long, metal rod is incredibly handy for reaching a dent from the inside, such as high in the front wing. Used with a hammer, most dents can be knocked out. Unfortunately, it isn't always possible to get to the back of a dent, either because some other component is in the way or the metal is double-skinned.

Use your small hammer to gradually tap in

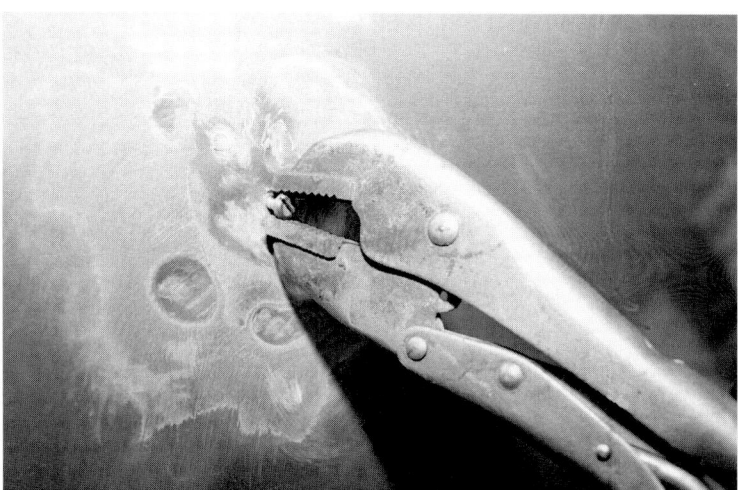

Light dents can be dressed back into place using a medium-weight hammer.

If there is no rear access, you can often pull out the worst part of a dent like this – a self-tapping screw in the metal and self-locking grips work wonders.

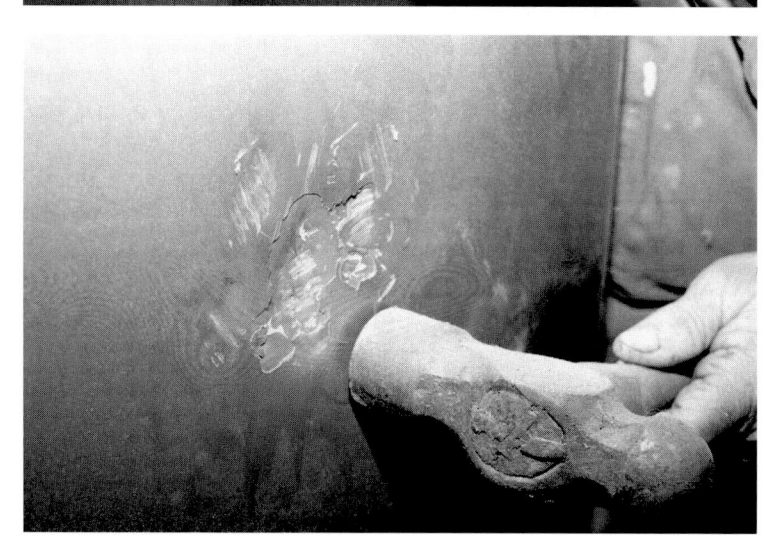

A reasonable finish is possible using two hammers – one on each side of the dent. The second hammer, obviously, is not visible.

When dealing with any body damage, the first step is to clean the area back to bare metal – and that goes for rust and dents.

Apply body filler in thin coats, gradually building up the surface.

the protruding creases on the outside and the centre of the dent should slowly work its way out. What you are doing, in effect, is reversing the sequence of the original damage. Think of it this way – another car, for example, hits your Mini, pushing the metal in and causing the edge of the dent to bow outwards, forming a series of creases. Tap in those creases and the dent all but disappears.

It does take a degree of confidence to attack bodywork with a hammer, but imagine somebody laying a piece of dented metal on your workbench and asking you to straighten it. You would know instinctively where and how to hit it.

When the metal has been restored to your satisfaction, lightly run a sanding disc (an electric drill and circular pad work well) over the surface to remove flaking paint and key the metal, ready to accept body filler.

If you have had to tap the metal from the inside, protect the newly exposed surface with a zinc-based paint, using an aerosol if necessary. Some purists fight shy of using filler, arguing that a car should be kept in its original state and what boils down to plastic is an unacceptable substitute for metal. Perhaps if I were working on a 1930s Lagonda or vintage Aston Martin I would accept that argument. But just consider these facts – modern body filler will not rust, if prepared properly it is indistinguishable from the original metal, and it effects a cheap and permanent repair.

Thoroughly mix the filler and hardener on a clean surface, such as a sheet of plywood or a ceramic tile, and use a small wallpaper scraper for the job. It is perfect. Follow the proportions recommended by the manufacturer, but do not be tempted to mix in extra hardener to speed up the curing process. It will go off more quickly, but it will also crack.

Apply the filler, using the plastic spreader provided, with thin coats, rather than trying to fill the dent in one go. When the contours seem about right, smooth off using 80-grit production paper and a rubbing block. Now run your fingers over the surface, feeling for high and low spots, apply more filler, rub down, feel the surface, and be prepared to carry out this routine maybe a dozen times until the finish is satisfactory.

When rubbing down, you may expose metal,

When the filler is standing proud of the metal, sand it flat. This is a DA (dual-action) air-driven sander, which is quick but gentle.

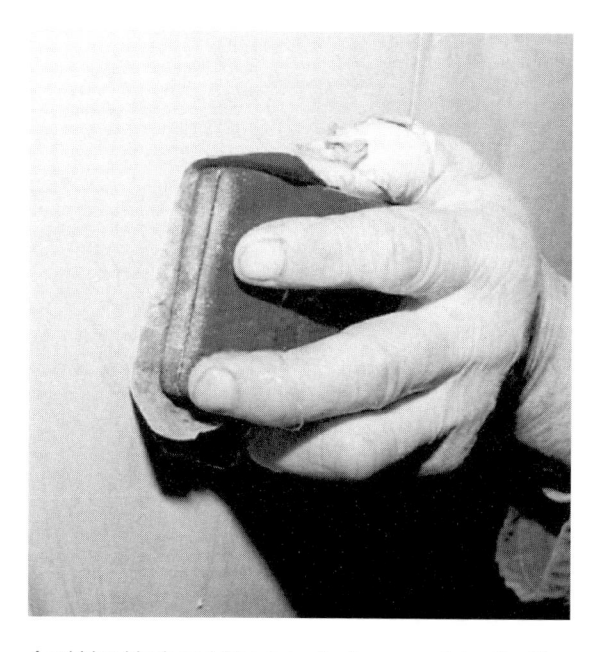

A rubbing block and 80-grit production paper bring the filler to near-perfect contours.

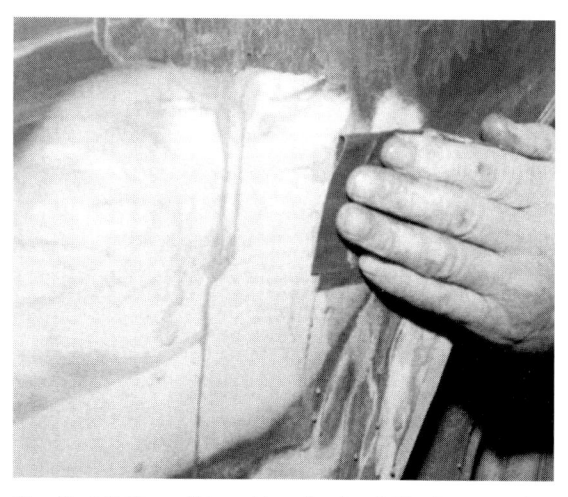

The final flatting-off is achieved using 800-grit wet-or-dry, used wet.

which means it is standing proud. Just tap it down slightly and apply more filler, using your rubbing block and 600-grit wet-or-dry to achieve a smoother finish and then finish off with 800-grit.

If the panel you are dealing with has attachments – such as a door handle or rear bumper – you need to know that the contour will match it. Before priming, refit the relevant component and make sure that the two mate correctly. Imagine the frustration, for example, of repairing a door panel and then refitting a handle only to find there is a gap between the two.

Remember, the effort devoted to preparation will have a direct result on the standard of the finished job. The more time and care you spend, the better the result will be. Many owners opt to use spray primer – either from an aerosol or a gun. I prefer to brush it on and there are good reasons. You can apply primer as thickly as you like with a brush, which will hide all manner of small imperfections. Just as importantly, modern fillers do tend to shrink (albeit slightly) when brought into contact with other chemicals (paint, in this case), but with a thick coat of primer, any signs of shrinkage will be lost. One coat of primer left for a day will give you the perfect base to flat off using 800-grit wet-or-dry.

The disadvantage of brush-priming is that rubbing it down requires proportionately more work, but the trade-off is well worthwhile. Primer is designed to dry slightly porous so that it will readily accept the colour coats. So avoid leaving your Mini exposed to the elements before the primer is painted over. When the primer is dry, feather in the edges so that the join is

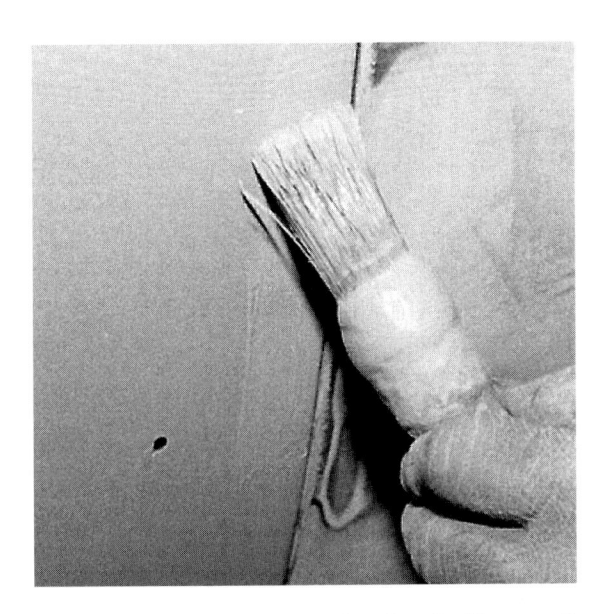

Brush-priming is the author's preferred method because it provides a thick layer on which to work later and covers a multitude of imperfections. The only drawback is the extra time which has to be taken in rubbing it down.

imperceptible. Even at this stage, you may need to apply more primer and flat it off once again.

Tackling corrosion

Dealing with rust damage requires a similar sort of approach to repairing dents, but first you must decide whether you actually want to tackle the corrosion or fit a new panel. Surface rust and scabs are no problem whatsoever. Thoroughly clean the panel with a sander (a drill attachment, as mentioned, is ideal) so that you are left with bright metal. Treat with a rust-converter and then prime.

But what if the rust has eaten through a panel? Well, it's now a case of judgment and weighing up what you are aiming to achieve. If the corrosion has caused pinholes the metal can be dished in with a hammer, treated with a rust-converter, filled and primed.

A larger hole, however, is a different matter. It can be repaired by grinding away rusted metal and bridging the hole with mesh and filler or, in extreme cases, glassfibre matting. But here is the part you might find unpalatable. When rust has taken a hold, you will never, ever stop it. Fact. By cutting out corroded metal and treating what is left with a rust-converter, you can slow down the process significantly, but you cannot stop it.

Repetition, I agree, but the point has to be emphasized because otherwise you will treat rust, be happy with the job, then find to your horror that it has popped through again within about a year. Even worse, the corrosion has been bubbling away beneath the surface and it is now worse than ever.

Replacement panels

So basically you have a choice. If you are content with keeping the corrosion as much under control as you can and effecting a permanent solution later, by all means use the mesh-and-filler approach. But if you intend to maintain your Mini in top order a new panel is the only answer. It took me years – and dozens of rust repairs which I thought were permanent – to reconcile myself to the situation.

Incidentally – and this should almost go without saying – never attempt to repair rust in a load-bearing structure such as a door sill or rear subframe. Replacement is the only route. Which brings us neatly to replacing panels.

Fitting a new bonnet or boot merely involves undoing a few bolts. One of the jobs you are most likely to encounter is replacing a front wing, and the first step is to buy the new one. You can then examine it, which will help you quickly realize where it is attached to the rest of the body and assist in the removal of the old item.

It can be cut away using an air chisel, driven by a compressor. These tools need care because they readily cut through sheet metal – often the bits you don't want to touch – and, as an unwanted bonus, create extremely sharp edges plus a most unholy and unneighbourly row. An angle-grinder is more friendly – and slightly quieter – and it allows you to work with greater precision.

Cut away the majority of the wing, leaving the edges. This will give you access to the spot-welds where it is joined to the inner wing, front panel and A-panel. Carefully grind through the welds and gradually pull the old wing clear.

Before fitting the new wing, you want to give it the best possible start in life, so treat the inner side with a decent rust-proofing agent, such as a zinc-based paint or – and the name often crops up – Hammerite. It has been around for years and lasts for years.

Offer the wing into position and temporarily fix it into place, either with two pairs of self-locking grips or a couple of blind rivets. Now make sure that the bonnet closes properly and the gap is even along the length of the wing and also the same as the opposite wing. You may find that a pattern-part will not be an exact fit – not uncommon – so a small amount of bending will be necessary.

It's here that a well-equipped workshop is necessary – that is, you will need a welder. The wing should be secured with a series of spot-welds about four inches apart. You can use an arc-welder, and although this provides an extremely strong joint, it is all too easy to blow right through the metal. A MIG welder is gentler, offers more control and does not distort the surrounding metal because the heat is localized. With the wing secured, once again check the fit with the bonnet. Satisfied? Then it is ready to be sprayed.

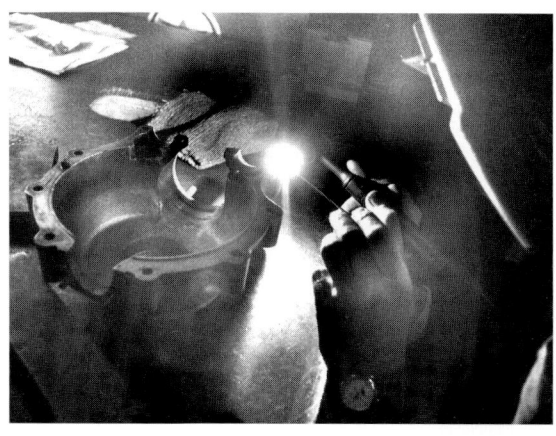

Another rust point on the Mini is the A-panel, which sits between the door and front wing. Once again, buy a new panel to study its contours and decide where it needs to be cut free from its attendant parts. Do the job piecemeal until all of the old panel has been removed.

Replacing the bonnet scuttle – that is, the panel which supports the top of the grille and bonnet-retaining mechanism – similarly involves cutting through the spot-welds and assuring correct alignment before it is welded into place. Some owners have got away with securing wings – and other panels, for that matter – by using either blind rivets or brazing. Neither is recommended because they do not offer the required strength.

Rusted door sills, as many Mini owners will tell you, are fairly common and also an MoT failure point. The quality of the welding is vital and I would not recommend that the home enthusiast tackles this job. If a wing came loose it would be annoying, but if a door sill did not have the strength and rigidity required of it the consequences in an accident could be serious. So leave this job to a professional unless you are 100

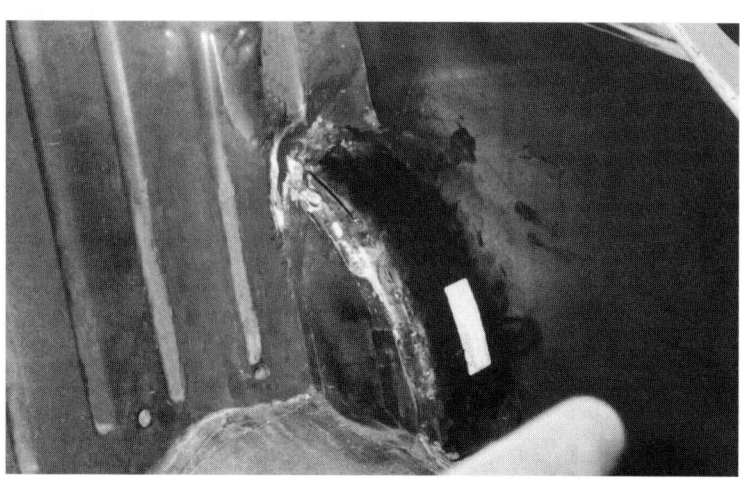

A MIG welder is a most invaluable piece of equipment, but always wear a mask because the rays are extremely harmful.

All manner of body repairs are within the scope of the home enthusiast with welding equipment, such as this inner rear wheelarch.

per cent confident of your welding ability.

So, your panel repairs/replacements are finished. Life becomes more interesting because applying the colour coats is an almost therapeutic exercise as you start to see your labour coming to fruition. But spraying is not without its problems and you have a few decisions to make.

First off, do you apply the paint so that it covers the repair only and then compound the panel so that old and new blend? Or do you respray the complete panel? For me, there is absolutely no choice to be made. Respraying a panel in its entirety eliminates the need for compounding and there is no chance that the paint will not match.

Of course, it might contrast with its adjacent panel because the original finish has faded, and there is nothing you can do about that (bar a complete respray). But at least you will not have conflicting colours on the same sheet of metal.

Respray techniques
The next decision is whether to use an aerosol or compressor and spray gun. It's all a matter of finance and personal circumstances. If you are unlikely to carry out future body repairs an aerosol will do fine. It just means that you will have to apply twice as many coats to achieve a large enough build-up of paint.

However, the committed fan of bodywork will choose a compressor and pukka gun, not the least of it being that you will now be in a position to carry out a total respray and also have the compressor for use with air-driven tools. I have used the full kit for years and never regretted the outlay.

And finally, with a gun, you then have a choice of different paint systems. They fall into three basic categories – cellulose, synthetic and two-pack (also referred to as 2K). Actually, there is a fourth, which is enamel, but that is reserved for cars which originally had that finish (1950s and earlier) and so is not relevant in our case.

Synthetic, as its name implies, is man-made and I am no great fan of it. It is rarely compatible with other systems and I have found that the standard of finish can be variable (possibly

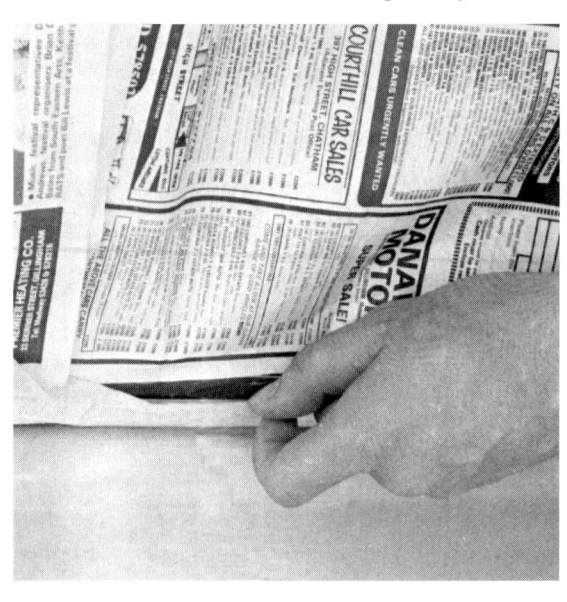

Newspaper is fine for masking off, but be careful not to tear it or get it wet, otherwise paint will seep through to exactly where you don't want it!

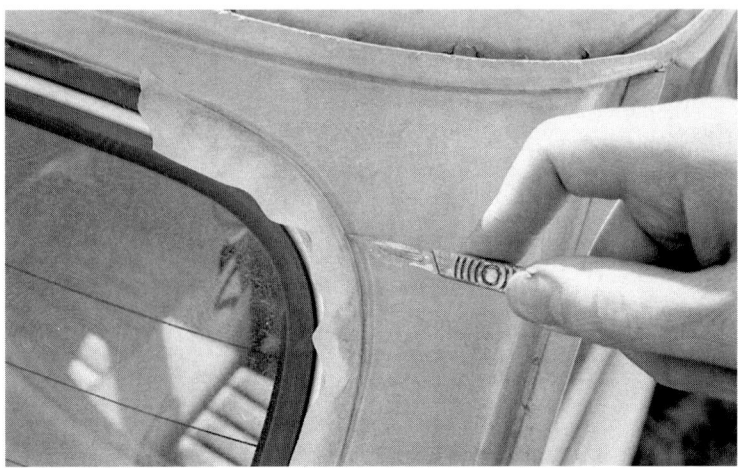

The masking tape can be finely trimmed with a modeller's knife.

The paint mix is important. Follow the manufacturer's instructions. Generally, a mix of 50-50 is ideal.

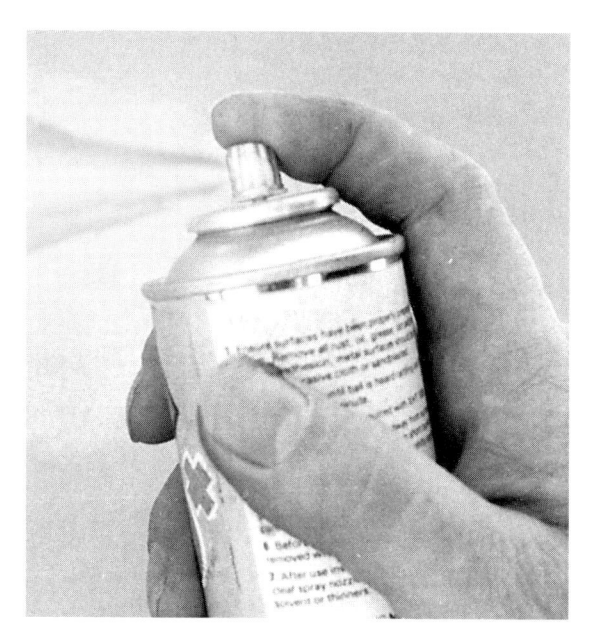

An aerosol is fine for painting one panel in isolation. However, you will need to apply several coats.

because of my lack of experience and patience).

Two-pack paint is ultra-tough and durable and the shine is almost unbelievable. But there are two drawbacks, the first being that such is the depth of shine that a Mini looks almost toy-like. Its paintwork has traditionally been subtle.

The other drawback – or perhaps I should say characteristic – is that two-pack is potentially dangerous. It contains iso-cyanates, which are a derivative of cyanide. No more need be said except that you need a good-quality air-fed mask for protection. Even some professionals do not like using two-pack because of its properties.

By the process of elimination, then, you will deduce that I favour cellulose. It is relatively harmless, easy to work with and, with care, will give you an original-looking finish. It is, of course, all a matter of opinion, and it must be said that some paint shop counter assistants will smirk when you ask for cellulose. Certain factions regard it as outdated. But it is still available and preferred by many enthusiasts of classic cars.

The panel to be sprayed must be rubbed down using 800-grit wet-or-dry until all traces of wax, dirt and imperfections have been removed and the paint has a matt finish. It should be masked off so that a surrounding area of at least 2 feet is covered to prevent overspray settling where you don't want it. It must be completely dry and free from dust or grease. Clean the surface with spirit wipe and follow up with a tack cloth. Both are available from bodywork shops.

I will describe the method of spraying using a gun and cellulose, but it is virtually identical to using an aerosol, except that you mix the paint yourself.

As mentioned earlier, a certain amount of mystique surrounds paint spraying, almost as if the sprayer is holding an artist's brush and bestowing his talents onto a canvas. But it is a skill rather than a gift, where a person requires precision rather than creativity. Which is why, of course, cars are painted by robots on the production line.

You have several variables to deal with, as follows – proportion of paint to thinners, air pressure, the speed the gun is moved, the distance the gun is held from the panel and the ambient temperature. Get them all correct and you are guaranteed an absolutely perfect finish.

Unless the manufacturer states otherwise, mix your paint and thinners 50–50. Buy the best

Using a gun requires practice. The technique is explained in the text.

quality thinners you can and choose the anti-bloom type to combat damp in the atmosphere. I spray using 50psi at the gun. Note that I said at the gun, rather than the pressure in the compressor's collector tank. You need a regulator valve in the airline to adjust this (all good compressors will be fitted with one).

The gun should be held between 6 and 8 inches from the panel. Spray from side to side and trigger-off briefly before making the return stroke to avoid a build-up of paint. Each coat should half overlap the last until the panel is covered.

As for speed of movement, the best way is to imagine your windscreen wipers on their lowest speed on a dry screen. Your gun should pass to and fro, but just the tiniest bit slower. Do not expect to achieve a good result with the first coat, or even the second or third. It might take up to six coats before the finish is acceptable. Allow each to cure thoroughly before the next is applied. After two coats, examine the surface for imperfections, such as pinholes, which can be dealt with using knifing stopper.

You will need to wait a couple of hours before the stopper can be rubbed down. If you have time to spare, apply three coats and then leave the paint overnight. This will allow it time to settle and for any shrinkage to occur. You then have a solid foundation of paint to flat off, ready for the final coats.

Once the final coat has been applied, do not be the slightest bit despondent if the finish is disappointing. What matters is that the paint is there and it can be suitably treated. Any runs or sags can be carefully rubbed away using 1200-grit

Here's one ready for the final coats.

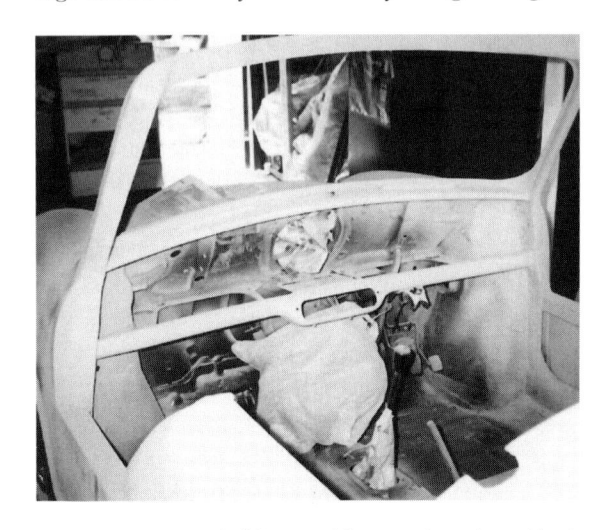

With a complete rebuild, everything needs to be rubbed down and primed in preparation for the colour coats.

wet-or-dry. Follow up with a rubbing compound and then good-quality polish.

As a quick troubleshooter, if the paint sags, either it is too thick, the gun was held too close, or it was not moved quickly enough. An orange-peel effect is caused by excessively thick paint. A thin mix (too much thinners) will cause runs or a matt finish. Moving the gun too quickly or holding it too far away will also lead to a flat finish.

If the new paint settles into pinholes – sometimes referred to as fisheyes – there is grease on the surface. If it cracks it is reacting to the original finish and a primer-sealer will have to be applied to isolate the surface.

So, you will have gathered that spraying is a skill to be learned by practice. Use an old sheet of metal to perfect your technique. It will eventually come as second nature. Just remember the basic rules: preparation plays an enormous part; it is always gratifying to get a good finish straight from the gun, but not vital thanks to modern rubbing compounds; and practice your technique so that the paint mix, the speed of the gun and the distance it is held from the panel work in harmony.

Earlier, I mentioned that ambient temperature is important. If you have a heated workshop that is not a problem. Otherwise, wait for a warm day or make sure that all draughts are excluded. No workshop? Well, provided the weather is reasonable you will get away with shielding the car with a makeshift shelter, fashioned from plastic sheeting. Provided it keeps the wind and dust from your Mini, the job will be possible.

Metallics

Metallic paint. No, I haven't forgotten it and the subject has been set aside until now because it warrants a small section of its own. Achieving a pleasing finish with metallics requires paying even more critical attention to detail. You will understand that when I explain how a metallic paint is given its effect.

Basically, it is ordinary paint which is mixed with tiny slivers of aluminium. Get them to lay flat and they act like thousands of tiny mirrors. But if they settle at an angle, or even upright and edge-on, that reflective quality is lost. Therefore, the pressure at the gun is especially important and the most common mistake is to spray when it is too high. About 45psi is the optimum. But be prepared to experiment to take into account the variations of paint from different manufacturers.

Metallic paint is thin and you will need at least half a dozen coats to build up a decent surface. Even then, it will not shine – regardless of polishing – until lacquer is applied. The system is called clear-over-base. That is, clear lacquer applied to the base coats.

It is under these circumstances that I have used two-pack lacquer. A cellulose lacquer also works well, but it is not so durable. In any event, provided the base coats have been applied correctly and they are free from runs or sags, you can lay on at least three coats of lacquer which can then be wet-flatted and polished as per normal paint, once cured. That includes the two-pack variety.

If you have repaired a dent, it is almost pointless trying to localize the spraying to a small area. The complete panel must be painted, otherwise the mismatch will be bordering on the awful. Such is the nature of metallics, even professionals have problems getting the right match.

Over the years, I have carried out something in the region of 200 resprays (on many cars, not just Minis) and the first jobs were, to put it frankly, abysmal. The finish was uncomfortably close to that of suede. But matters progressed when I began paying more attention to preparation, rather than rushing to apply the colour coats, and when I realized that there was a great deal which could be done to paint once it was on and cured. Above all, I wasn't frightened to have a go and it has paid dividends.

With that in mind, do not fight shy of a complete respray. It merely involves everything explained so far, except that there is more of it. Every panel must be rubbed down using 800-grit

Rear subframe removal is made simpler with the car jacked well up and firmly supported.

With the rear raised and supported and everything disconnected, the rear subframe can be lowered and pulled clear.

to remove dirt and small surface imperfections and, of course, the whole car needs to be masked off.

Spray in this sequence – (1) roof, (2) bottom of front wing upwards, over the bonnet and over the opposite wing, (3) one side, (4) the other side, (5) the rear end. One gun-full of paint will see you cover the whole car. This means that you will not need to stop halfway through to refill the gun and, therefore, you should not get any unsightly joins.

If your Mini has a number of small scratches and scabs and the paint is old, tackle a complete paint job. At worst, it will have cost you 2 litres of paint, a can of thinners, a few sundries such as masking tape and some of your spare time.

At best, the finished job will transform the look of your car. I cannot stress sufficiently that, provided there is enough paint to work with – up to half a dozen coats – by progressively using 1200-grit wet-or-dry, a rubbing compound and then polish, you will at least be pleased and at best delighted with the results.

Perhaps the most profound comment my panel-beater friend made was this – paintwork does not need to be perfect, just look perfect. There is a world of difference.

Rear subframe

If you run an ageing Mini, are unlucky, or both you will be faced with replacing the rear subframe. It is by no means a technically taxing task, just awkward, mucky and time-consuming.

The rear will need to be jacked up and supported (obviously not under the subframe) and then the various components removed, such as brake lines, handbrake cable, fuel pump (if appropriate), shock absorbers and exhaust. When the subframe has been laid bare, undo the four main retaining nuts and away it comes. If the threads are tight, liberally soak them with a penetrating fluid and allow to soak in overnight.

Prevention is always better than cure, of course, and the longer you can keep rust at bay, the better. If you want to make a really thorough job, have the underside steam-cleaned. It's not an expensive exercise and will save you absolutely hours of work.

Underbody sealant was once in vogue for rust protection and it does work well. However, over a period of time, the sealant loses its rubbery properties and eventually cracks. Water can get trapped between the sealant and body and corrosion will set in. So if you do opt for this type of sealant – and the advantages are that it is cheap and easily applied with a brush – check it once a year and touch in sections of metal which have become exposed.

Another effective means of guarding against corrosion is to use a kit, usually comprising a pump-applicator, lance and the substance itself. Typically, it will be an oil-based solution, which is designed to keep out the elements and adhere well to metal surfaces. The underside should be thoroughly sprayed and box-sections drilled and filled with the chemical and then the holes plugged with rubber bungs.

Several types of rust-proofing kits are on the market and they all seem to work well. Alternatively, you can have the job carried out professionally. Significantly more expensive, but a reputable company will guarantee against corrosion for several years and the documentation backing up that promise is a good selling point.

Naturally, the subframe should be similarly treated – either with underbody sealant or a proprietary rust-proofing kit – and you are advised to take matters a stage further if fitting a new item. Apply a thick coat of a zinc-based paint and then follow up with the protective medium of your choice.

This is the front subframe assembly. It is a sight you will rarely – if ever – see because this component is not known to rust, due to protection by oil mist from the engine.

The author built a Mini from a brand-new bodyshell. It was just as easy to lift the shell over the front subframe as to offer that component into position. The chap flexing his muscles is not, it should be pointed out, the author.

CHAPTER 10

The interior

Time to repair or time to replace

EARLIER, in the section on buying Minis, I suggested that you should split – metaphorically speaking – a car into three main categories – the mechanicals, bodywork and the interior. With three distinct areas to consider, you can then make up your mind whether a car is worth buying, and the chances are that the interior will have a major bearing on your decision. So the need to keep it in good condition should be obvious. Quite apart from maintaining resale value, a smart interior will increase your driving pleasure.

Prevention is very much the keyword because damage to seats or items of trim is not easy to repair. So it's a case of avoiding smoking, spillages and any other activity which will ruin fabric and vinyl. Seat covers are an excellent idea although they are visually self-defeating because you will never get to see the interior as it was meant to look.

Many proprietary cleaners are available commercially and one of the best is the foam cleaner, similar to the type you would use for clothing. Spray it on, let it dry and brush or vacuum off. It works beautifully with fabric-covered seats.

With deep stains, the seat may need a thorough wash with detergent which will soak the foam base. Remove the seat from your Mini, which, although requiring extra work, will allow you to use liberal amounts of water, then let the foam and fabric dry naturally without creating a dank smell inside.

The real problem comes, of course, when a seat is either torn or bears the scar of a cigarette burn. The ultimate answer is to let a professional coachtrimmer effect a repair because, with the best will in the world, an amateur will never achieve a perfect result. To put matters into perspective, the apprenticeship for a coach-trimmer is at least five years and many to whom I have spoken say they continue to learn long after that period.

But let's be realistic (and some might say brutal). Although a Mini is a desirable car, it is not in the same league as, say, a classic Jaguar, Aston Martin or Rolls-Royce, when perfection and originality are sacrosanct. You want your Mini to be smart, but the chances are that it will serve as everyday, practical transport and cost will be a consideration. Therefore, you will have to compromise, although that doesn't mean accepting that a repair should be shoddy.

Vinyl can split or crack and applying a patch is the answer. Specialist coachtrimmers supply repair kits and, at worst, you can cut out a small patch from an area which does not show, such as underneath the seat squab.

Fabric seats, however, are harder to repair. Once again, consult a specialist supplier because

When buying a Mini, pay attention to the interior because it is not easy to put right should there be a problem. This is a somewhat extreme case of what to avoid.

one of the latest innovations is a kit to deal with velour. You add small strands of fabric until the best match possible is obtained. Alternatively, cut out a small patch from a hidden area and stick it into place, using a fabric adhesive, which dries colourless.

Another option is to buy a secondhand seat, either through a club or at an autojumble. There is naturally the choice of buying new from a main dealer. But actually sourcing the material and then fitting it will prove difficult. So you will by now have amply taken the point that preserving seats is far preferable to repairing them.

The headlining, however and perhaps surprisingly, is easier to deal with. It's held in place with a series of rods which form a framework, which is not difficult to remove. But fitting it requires care because unless tensioned correctly, you will end up with unsightly sagging.

Carpets hardly deserve a mention, with all due respect, because complete kits are readily available and at most reasonable prices. You might well consider fitting sound-deadening material, available from specialists, because the Mini has never been noted for its silence.

One of the most irritating problems which can affect an interior is an ingress of water. Irritating in the sense that pinpointing exactly where it is getting in defies all attempts. The trouble is that water could be seeping in so gradually that you would never know its route, but the build-up causes damp carpets and the resultant smell. If the heater is not leaking, clearly, water must be entering from outside of the car. So let's continue that logic and use it as a basis for diagnosis.

If you exaggerate the situation, all should become clear. First, sprinkle a light coating of talcum powder on the carpets. Now close the doors and windows and aim a hose at your Mini, letting the jet of water hit it from all directions. Wait a few minutes for excess water to drain from the bodywork and then carefully inspect the interior. The path of the water will be clearly recorded by the talcum powder, which, as a bonus, is both fragrant and easy to vacuum up.

Even later Minis have a relatively spartan interior and there is much you can do to add character. Put these items on your shopping list – a set of rally-style seats with colour-coded mats, aluminium-spoked steering wheel, full-width dash and a few extra instruments, such as rev-counter and ammeter, centre console and either aluminium or leather-bound gear-lever knob. That package – and it's been favoured by many – will increase the driving experience immeasurably.

The subtle approach can make a big difference – like here, with the addition of a dash-mounted rev-counter and sports steering wheel.

CHAPTER 11

Upgrading your Mini

Sensible modifications for reliability, performance improvement and sheer driving pleasure

THE MINI has a huge advantage over many other cars, which is its simplicity. The point being that because it is so basic, in relative terms, the field is left wide open for improvements and modifications. And because the Mini is so popular, the market is positively bristling with components, which will enable you to enhance just about every aspect of its character, from appearance to performance.

If you stripped down a modern engine – say, from a car two or three years old – and then dismantled an A-Series unit and laid out the parts on a bench, one thing would be apparent. That is, there is very little difference in principle between the two.

Obviously, technology has improved over the years, along with engine design – overhead camshafts and four-valve cylinder heads are now the norm rather than the exception – but the concept of the reciprocating engine has remained virtually the same. Four (or whatever is the case) cylinders going up and down in their bores and spinning a crankshaft.

What the manufacturers have done is to improve the ancillaries, such as the ignition and cooling systems. And that is the route you can take with the Mini. The A-Series engine is fine in itself and will be long-lived with regular servicing. Modify a few of the components and you can only add to its reliability.

Contactless ignition
An excellent first step is to fit a contactless ignition system. Now this will appear to fly in the face of what I said in the ignition section, when contact breakers were extolled for their simplicity. The point I was making then was that there is absolutely nothing wrong with contact breakers provided they are correctly and regularly maintained. I also said that one definite advantage is that fault-finding and cure are simple.

Well, I stand by that. However, a good-quality aftermarket ignition kit is a worthwhile investment because it will improve starting – even if only marginally – and remove the need for maintenance. Typically, these kits have an electronic sensor which fits in place of the points and a disc with cut-outs (usually referred to as a chopper) which rotates between the sensor's eyes (for want of a better description). It interrupts current to produce sparks, just as points open to do the same thing.

A contactless set-up does not need adjusting and because there is no mechanical contact, it will take wear in the distributor bearings into account, thus all but eliminating timing scatter.

The most basic kit will provide you with a sensor, chopper and new base plate. You can take matters further with a booster pack, or amplifier, which will strengthen the spark. Whatever the choice, I would retain the original base plate and

The most sought-after of them all – the Cooper. Can't afford one? Then carefully modify your engine to reap similar power outputs.

points and keep them in my toolkit so, should the new system break down (and if it does, you will not be able to sort it out at the roadside), you can quickly revert to points to get you out of trouble.

That is not a vote of no-confidence in aftermarket contactless ignition kits, just the acceptance of reality that they can give trouble, albeit extremely rarely, and a DIY repair is not usually possible.

Electric fan

You might consider fitting an electric fan to replace the mechanical version. They offer two advantages, and the first is allowing the engine to run at maximum efficiency. A mechanical fan spins all the time, regardless of whether it is needed. However, an electric fan is controlled by a thermostat, which means that the engine is allowed to reach its correct running temperature as quickly as possible and the fan comes into play only when it is needed.

The second advantage is that an electric fan saves fuel because it does not unnecessarily sap power. Your initial reaction is probably that a mechanical fan requires very little effort to spin. Well, that is true to an extent. But, without going into complicated mathematical formulae, the faster it turns, the greater the required effort becomes. In fact at maximum revs a fan can use up to 3bhp. Admittedly, this is not a massive amount of power, and equally, a Mini's fuel consumption is so frugal that if you lose the odd mpg here and there it is hardly the end of the world. But taking all things into account, an electric fan is a sensible move and it will also keep your Mini just that little bit cooler in heavy traffic.

During the course of my dealings with Minis I have come across a rubber-belt conversion for the camshaft. It replaces the original chain and sprockets and runs dry. These belts are extremely tough and also operate silently. Additionally, they require no lubrication and therefore there is no chance of an oil leak.

This conversion has been reasonably well proven, but you will have to scour the marketplace because it has never been given such a high profile as, say, engine performance components and may take some tracking down.

To me, a contactless ignition set, electric fan and possibly belt-drive conversion for the camshaft would be enough. I would follow that up with a halogen conversion for the headlights and be quite happy with those modifications as a basic exercise in updating.

Unleaded fuel

Then, of course, the question of unleaded fuel must pose itself, and it is a question which continues to vex owners and divide opinions. Minis built up to October 1988 (as delivered from the factory, not when first registered) were designed to burn leaded petrol. Unleaded fuel can damage the valve seats because it does not contain the lead content necessary to protect them. You will notice that I used the word 'can' rather than 'will' and this is based on personal experience.

I have yet to read the definitive work on unleaded fuel, which is the result of comprehensive, long-term and independent scientific tests. The reason such tests have never been carried out is, I strongly suspect, that there are so many conflicting interests. Fuel companies would hardly want to damage sales or reputations by vaunting the problems of unleaded petrol. On the other hand, companies carrying out lead-free conversions to cylinder heads would hardly be boosting business by playing down the potential consequences of using unleaded petrol. Just to complicate the equation, the environmental movement is firmly opposed to air pollution – and rightly so – and anything which can be said in favour of unleaded fuel is useful ammunition.

So exactly where do you stand? Well, it depends to a large extent on mileage. Valve seat recession happens over a fairly long period, and if you are a short-journey person there is every chance that your valve seats will last for a great deal of time. All you need do is check the valve clearances at every major service to see if the gap has closed significantly. If they are more than a thou tighter than at the last service, leave matters for 3000 or so miles and check the clearances again to see if they have closed up further.

If they have, you know that the seats are suffering and you will need a lead-free conversion – that is, new valve seats. If not, just carry on motoring with lead-free fuel and if there is a tendency for the engine to pink, retard the ignition just a touch to eliminate it.

Just to further complicate matters, the fuel market is subject to change, and while at the time of writing LRP (lead replacement petrol) is available, and most of the major manufacturers offer additives, the situation could alter at any time. So my advice is to use LRP or an additive and regularly check the valve clearances. If you cover a fairly high mileage and/or plan to keep your Mini for some time, opt for a lead-free converted cylinder head (incidentally, the official factory converted cylinder head has the letter 'U' stamped between the engine prefix and start of the serial number).

On a point of interest rather than information, the quality of fuel in the 1930s and 1940s was extremely poor and it did not contain lead. Yet I have never heard of cars from that era suffering from valve seat recession. Presumably there are factors involved to which I am not privy.

Performance tuning
Considering that the Mini was designed as a runabout – albeit a rather chic runabout – it has attracted a cult following by performance

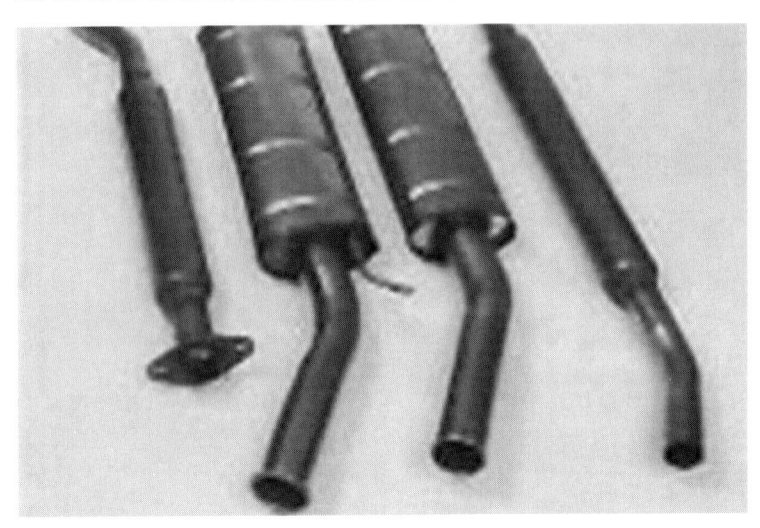

One of the first steps in Mini tuning is to let the exhaust breathe more freely.

enthusiasts, not the least of it being inspired by the rally successes of the 1960s and the aura created by the Cooper and Cooper S.

The A-Series engine just begs to be tuned so that performance can start to get on a par with that amazing handling and manoeuvrability inherent to the design. At the start of this chapter I referred to making sensible modifications, and that is the key. Be sensible rather than radical and you will be rewarded.

The engine's tuning potential is quite incredible and with a maximum overbore, special block and long-throw crankshaft, the capacity can be taken out to nearly 1500cc. Such an engine, with the appropriate ancillaries, would provide phenomenal power. It would also be an expensive exercise and leave you with a somewhat fragile powerplant with a love for the open road, but definite dislike for traffic. An extreme example, agreed, but I needed to make the point that you are looking for a Mini with a satisfying gain in performance, but still blessed with reliability and a relatively sweet nature.

Approaching the subject of tuning for performance can cause confusion, partly because of the embarrassment of choices on offer from specialists. But remember this, it doesn't matter how shiny and well-packaged any of the products is – and that takes in everything from carburettors to large-bore exhausts – the object of the exercise is exactly the same: to improve engine efficiency. You want to get as much fuel/air into the combustion chamber as quickly as possible and for it to burn and exit with the minimum of delay. It is no more complicated than that. So you will gather, then, that extra performance relies almost 100 per cent on getting your Mini's engine to breathe as efficiently as possible.

Power tuning will impose extra stresses on your engine, so before considering anything but the mildest of tweaks, you need a sound basis on which to work. That is, an engine with good oil pressure and sound compression readings. These factors are not so much dependent on mileage as regular maintenance over the years (such is the virtue of frequent oil and filter changes).

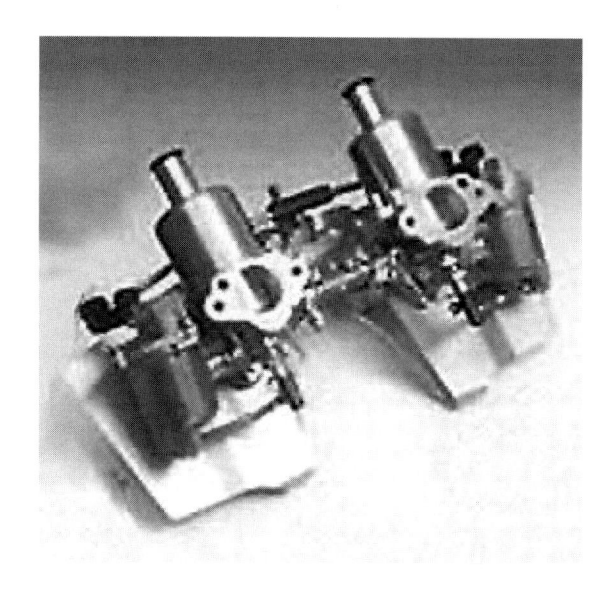

Twin SU carburettors offer useful performance gains and are totally in keeping with Mini lore – that is, Cooper versions. However, they do need to be kept in tune.

And at the risk of disappointing owners of 850cc models, I would not bother trying to extract extra power from these engines because, frankly, they do not have enough cubic capacity in the first place. Of course, they can be tuned, but why bother when fitting a 1000cc-or-upwards engine will give you an immediate increase in performance and have the potential for even more?

It has to be said that the 1275cc engine is the best motor on which to carry out your tuning exercise for the simple reason that it has the largest capacity. But the 1000cc and 1100cc motors will respond to modifications, even if they will never ultimately offer the potential of the 1275.

So exactly where do you start? Well, it depends on exactly what you are aiming for. The approach to adopt is to fit aftermarket components in a logical order so that each paves the way for the next and, luckily, there is a set procedure for the Mini, regardless of engine size, which has been widely recognized and adopted.

The simplest first step is to fit a free-flow air filter, and at the risk of sounding blatantly biased, the name K & N must spring to mind. They use a foam element which allows an almost

A modified cylinder head is an important part in the quest for extra power. They come in various stages of tune (see text).

unrestricted flow of air. The power gains are not vast, but you have now set the scene for a better breathing engine.

The next move is to turn your attention to the exhaust system. At the very least, fit a performance tail-box. This will give you 2 or 3bhp extra and also provide emotional horsepower. It comes with the sound.

The Mini's exhaust manifold is almost laughable in its inefficiency. A dreadful cast-iron affair which is as adept at strangulation as it is in allowing exhaust gases to pass through. To make matters worse, it is integral with the inlet manifold so you cannot replace it in isolation. Tuning specialists can solve that by supplying you with free-flow inlet and exhaust manifolds in one piece or as individual items. Some kits require you to separate the originals with a hacksaw so that the performance exhaust manifold can then be fitted. On balance, I would opt for the complete kit – that is, performance inlet and exhaust manifolds bought as a pair, which will improve breathing considerably.

Exhaust manifolds usually come in two variants – four-into-one or four-into-two-into-one and each has its own characteristics. The former will provide more power higher up the rev range, while the latter increases mid-range torque. The supplier will advise. Personally, mid-range torque is what I would be looking for.

So how far have we come? Well, with a free-flow air filter, less-restrictive manifolds and performance exhaust system, you can expect about 12 per cent more power, plus noticeably improved throttle response.

Next on your hit-list is the carburettor. The SU is a versatile instrument and because it does not rely on fixed jets, the mixture can be adjusted quite extensively throughout the range of throttle openings, giving you reasonably generous extra helpings of fuel. Nevertheless, to take advantage of the modifications so far, fitting a needle-and-jet kit will reap benefits, which is a cheap and simple means of boosting power. Performance-enhanced versions of the HS2 and HS4 carbs are available from specialists and they will provide a few extra bhp compared with a needle-and-jet kit.

Alternatively, you might consider fitting a completely different carburettor, which will give significant gains, and it all depends on how far your tuning exercise is to extend. A twin-choke progressive carburettor is much favoured (Weber 28/36 or its equivalent) because it works well and is also easy to keep in tune.

Basically, these carbs have two chokes. The primary choke is opened by the initial throttle movement and then, when the engine demands more fuel, the secondary, and larger, choke is opened by a mechanical linkage. So you have the advantages of a twin-carburettor set-up, but

The ultimate in fuel delivery for a roadgoing Mini – a sidedraught Weber carburettor.

without the rigmarole of keeping them in tune. On top of that, the secondary choke comes into play only on demand, which helps fuel consumption if you treat the throttle with respect.

As for fitting twin carburettors, they will obviously provide a useful power increase and also be in keeping with the performance stablemates, the Cooper versions. Their only drawback is that they are a little finicky and will require fairly frequent tuning. So it is a trade-off for you to make – a twin-choke instrument which is simple to tune or twin carbs, which will provide a little more power but demand more frequent attention.

I ran a Cooper S for a couple of years which already had a Weber 28/36 conversion and was more than pleased with the performance and its delightful habit of staying in tune. Perhaps the only fault I could find was its lack of originality. So, if I were tuning, say, a Clubman or 1275GT then a twin-choke progressive carburettor would be high on, if not top of, my shopping list, especially since originality would not be such an issue as with the likes of a Cooper.

No more need be done in the carburation department at this juncture because, basically, the standard head and camshaft would not be able to take advantage of any more fuel-air delivery than is already available. Instead, the next item to consider is the cylinder head. And conveniently, if you are going to fit a reworked head then make sure it has already been converted to run on lead-free petrol, thus doing two jobs in one.

Stage by stage
You have probably read extracts from tuning manuals and specialists' catalogues about various stages of tune regarding cylinder heads and it can get a little tangled. But by and large, it goes like this: a stage one head has been gas-flowed and the ports have been balanced so that they are equal in size; a stage two head will have been flowed and fitted with larger inlet valves; and a stage three head will also have larger exhaust valves.

Just occasionally, a tuner will offer a stage four head, that is one which has been skimmed to increase the compression ratio. I have always been happy with the standard CR, especially with today's fuels and their tendency to make engines pink.

In terms of power, a stage one head is worth about an extra 6 to 8 brake horsepower, while stage two gives you 3 or 4bhp more on top of that. Stage three is worth a similar gain.

Of course, you can rework your cylinder

The camshaft has a bigger effect on an engine's characteristics than any other component. Choose carefully and, perhaps, consider a performance distributor.

head yourself, but restrict the treatment to cleaning up the ports by removing as little metal as possible and getting them as even in shape and size as you can. For a decent performance gain, it is infinitely preferable to leave the job to a professional because head technology is an incredibly complex subject, which has gradually evolved over the years, mainly through trial and error.

Four decades or so ago, it was generally thought that large ports with a mirror finish provided the ultimate in cylinder head tuning. And there was no argument that they certainly allowed the mixture to flow in copious quantities. With the advent of flow meters, engine tuners realized that although the mixture was arriving very quickly, the size of the ports had a direct effect on gas speed. Large ports meant it flowed swiftly at high revs, but the speed decreased mid-range (very much like squeezing the end of a hosepipe – the smaller the exit, the stronger the jet). And that, of course, reduced torque where it was needed the most.

On top of that, tuners also realized that the fuel-air mix could actually flow too quickly, which meant that some of it passed straight through without being burnt. That brought valve overlap into the equation.

Another factor came to light, and that was the need for turbulence. In simple terms, a head needed to have the effect of swirling the fuel and air to make it mix thoroughly. Imagine stirring thick coffee with milk on top and then suddenly holding the spoon still. That would cause the milk and coffee to collide, as it were, and mix properly. A mirror finish port would never achieve this and the new way of thinking was to leave the port smooth, but unpolished, to help the fuel and air tumble over each other and mix well.

Some tuners took it a stage further with what they termed a wayform interruptor. That is, a small step in the inlet ports which deliberately stood in the way of the mixture and caused turbulence. Somewhat academic points, I will concede, but they will go some way to help you understand just how much skill and precision is involved in tuning a cylinder head for optimum performance.

When your head has been modified, you can now think about more fuel-air delivery and a 40mm sidedraught carburettor should be treated as just about the ultimate for a roadgoing Mini (a Weber 40DCOE or its equivalent). Some enthusiasts have fitted a 45mm carburettor, but that is really overdoing matters because you will never need that volume of delivery for the road. A 40mm sidedraught carb will provide ample fuel and then even more for a road Mini. However, be prepared for induction roar – it is quite considerable with this instrument.

The final link in the performance-tuning chain is the camshaft, and it has been deliberately left until last. The reason is that on most engines, and on the Mini in particular, fitting a performance cam will be of little if any benefit unless the rest of the system has been tuned. In some cases, it will actually detract from performance.

Bear in mind that the camshaft has a bigger effect on the engine's power characteristics than any other single component. As with cylinder heads, tuning companies have their own pet names for cams, and you will come across descriptions such as fast road, rally, half race and full race. The profiles vary, but generally it's the fast road camshaft you are after. Check the specifications and every reputable manufacturer will be able to tell you exactly what each profile of cam will offer. That is, where power and torque increases will fall in the rev range and also, how the tickover will be affected. These are all extremely important points because, for normal use, a cam which gives a significant power increase beyond 5000rpm and makes the tickover lumpy at anything below 1500rpm is quite obviously not a practical proposition. I would look for a camshaft which allowed a steady tickover at no more than 1000rpm, and preferably a little lower, and one which produced more torque and power between 2500rpm and 5000rpm – the rev range in which your engine will spend most of its time. Also, check with the manufacturer about noise. Some performance camshafts do not have a quietening ramp and they cause a noticeable clatter.

The amount of effort and money you could spend tuning a Mini engine is phenomenal – balanced bottom end, roller-rockers, sodium-filled valves, vernier timing gear, the list goes on. But to remind you of the purpose of this section, the accent is very heavily on sensible modifications which will bless your Mini with an engine which not only offers zippy performance, but is also reliable, tractable and fun to drive.

It is something of an urban myth that a tuned engine uses more petrol. Performance tuning is, as stated, tuning for efficiency, and a more efficient engine uses less fuel. It is only if you take full advantage of the extra performance that fuel consumption will increase. Drive it gently and economy will actually improve.

All performance parts must work in harmony with each other, and for that reason it is best to buy your components from one firm which (a) has built itself a reputation for quality and expertise, and (b) will have developed its products alongside each other so that they are known to work well together.

As for a complete package, here is my ideal

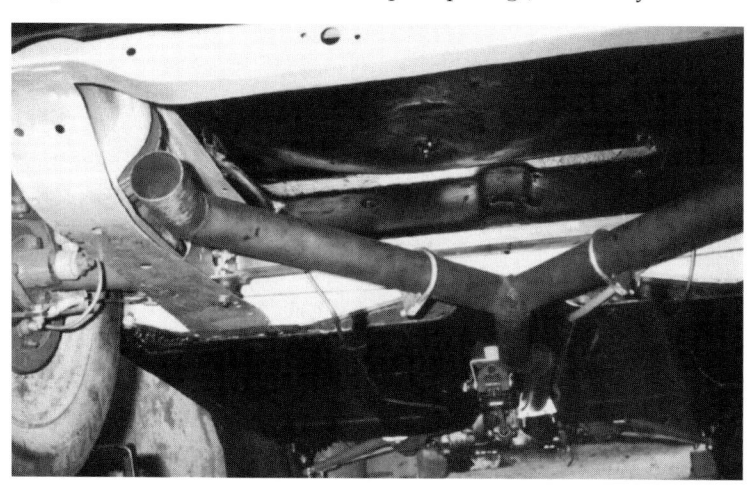

A twin-exhaust system will provide very little – if any – extra power above that offered by a single pipe. However, the visual effect is quite pronounced and the noise encouraging!

tuning set-up for a roadgoing Mini engine: free-flow air filter; performance exhaust system; performance inlet-exhaust manifold; carb conversion, preferably a twin-choke progressive instrument; stage two cylinder head; and fast road camshaft.

This set-up will give you a power increase in the region of 25 per cent which, for the 1275GT, puts you at least on a par with a Cooper S, albeit without the aura that goes with the name.

Money spent on the rolling road is money well spent. If you have embarked on a tuning exercise to the extent of that just mentioned, book a session on a dynamometer. An expert operator will be able to check the mixture and timing throughout the rev range and adjust matters accordingly, removing any guesswork and providing you with the best possible settings.

Wheels, tyres, brakes and suspension
The Mini is fabled for its roadholding, and even in standard form and with the bottom-of-the-range models, its surefootedness is commendable. Nevertheless, it can be improved, and one of the most popular means of enhancing road manners – not to mention appearances – is a set of alloy wheels.

Aesthetics aside, alloy wheels offer one big advantage over their steel counterparts and that is their lighter weight. Anything which is not controlled by the suspension is termed unsprung weight which, basically, means it has a free hand to do whatever it likes, which can have an effect on the handling. Reduce that weight and the effect is smaller. The wheels fall into that category and four alloys, compared with four steel rims, offer a useful weight-saving. They also increase steering responsiveness and their only main drawback is that they are delicate and easy to damage on kerbs.

As for fitting wider rims, well, that is largely a matter of personal taste. I wouldn't go wider than 5.5J. In fact, 5J is wide enough for me. It depends what look you are aiming to achieve and whether you wish to fit extended wheelarches, which will either have to be secured with self-tapping screws or blind rivets and then sprayed, depending on the type you choose.

Fortunately, whereas a few years ago you would have needed to work out the inset and offset of a rim (the inset is the distance between the centre and inside edge of the rim and the offset to the outer edge of the rim) to make sure that it would not foul the bodywork, all you need do now is pick your style of rim and then specify it for a Mini.

With a pretty vast choice of rim sizes and styles has come an equally vast choice of tyres and it is the aspect ratio which has the most dramatic visual effect. The aspect ratio is signified

Wider arches and alloy wheels benefit handling and looks alike. The choice of wheels is enormous and manufacturers have now taken any guesswork out of the equation.

The Cooper engine – complete with twin SUs – is the ultimate incarnation of the Mini's powerplant. However, it is not too difficult to bring a standard motor up to – or at least near – the Cooper's specifications.

by the series of tyre. For example, a 75-series tyre has a wall height which is three-quarters (75 per cent) of its width. Put into more understandable terms, a 100-series tyre (which to my knowledge, does not exist, at least not for cars in the modern era) would have a square profile.

The Mini is fitted with a 70-series tyre as standard (apart from the short-lived Denovo wheels) which means that the wall height is 70 per cent of the width. That is a fair compromise between comfort and handling. Reduce the aspect ratio and, as the walls become smaller in height, so their rigidity increases. This means that there is very little roll on corners. But the lower you go, the harsher the ride becomes.

A little while back, a 55-series tyre was considered ultra-low profile. Now, you can go as low as 50-series, which are little more than glorified elastic bands. The effect on appearance is stunning, it has to be said, but the ride is almost unbearable, unless you are super-tough and put handling above any other creature comfort.

Something else might have occurred to you – the smaller the aspect ratio, the smaller the diameter. Which, of course, will effect overall gearing. This will increase fuel consumption and also make your speedo reading inaccurate. Well, there is a way round these problems. For every 10 per cent drop in aspect ratio, increase the wheel diameter by an inch. For example, a standard Mini with 10-inch wheels and 70-series tyres will have appproximately the same gearing as a car with 11-inch wheels and 60-series tyres. It is by no means a precise science, but close enough to be acceptable.

I appreciate that 11-inch wheels are hardly commonplace, but these figures are given as examples. As I said, the wheel and tyre manufacturers have all of the necessary specifications so there is no guesswork involved and it largely depends on your choice of wheel width (obviously, the width has a bearing on the aspect ratio). For the record, I would not drop below a 60-series tyre, bearing in mind that the comfort factor on a standard Mini is not one of its strong points.

The suspension department can be dealt with fairly briefly. Various lowering kits are available and I would never drop a Mini more than an inch for fear of scuffing the tyres on the inner bodywork should the suspension bottom out (quite easy with four occupants and a bumpy road). Instead, I would limit my work to replacing the shock absorbers with uprated items, designed for road rather than track use.

Disc-braked Minis are fine to start with because, in keeping with most cars, the brakes have a degree of over-engineering built in from the start. Just make sure that the system is in tip-top order.

Even the Cooper's dash layout is spartan with not even a rev-counter. Consequently, it is open to improvement.

As for drum brakes, well, they are not recommended for a tuned Mini and will quickly fade with repeated hard use. This can be overcome by fitting competition linings, although they are temperamental for road use. If you are considering tuning a Mini, go for a disc-braked model at the outset. If it is too late and you already own one with drum brakes, consider a conversion, and that would involve cannibalizing another Mini for all the relevant parts – discs, calipers, stub axles, etc.

On a final note, whatever modifications you make should be passed on to your insurance company. Failure to let them know could invalidate your policy.

So what is my ultimate Mini? A combination of many facets and factors discussed in this book. It would feature an engine tuned to the specifications mentioned a little earlier (carb, exhaust and fuel system, reworked head and fast road cam, preferably on a 1275), contactless ignition, uprated shock absorbers, alloy wheels with 60-series tyres, full-width dash, rally-style seats and alloy-spoked steering wheel. I would also fit uprated universal joints (the needle-roller type), uprated bushes in the engine stabilizers, the cooling mods as mentioned, a halogen headlight conversion and a good burglar alarm! I would also want a service book which told me that the oil and filter had been changed every 6000 miles. Simple, effective, understated and immensely enjoyable. Which, in a few words, neatly sums up the Mini.

It is the embellishments which can ultimately make or break the appearance of your Mini, and by that I mean the brightwork. Lightly-pitted chrome might respond to a good-quality polish. If not then apply the polish with wire wool rather than cloth. Do not be tempted to use a nylon scourer because that is actually harder than the plating and will score it noticeably. If the rust is deep, buy new components because, comparing the price of items such as bumpers and headlight surrounds with having them rechromed, there really is no contest.

Die-cast alloys, such as door handles, are prone to pitting and if the wire wool treatment fails to work then once again, buy new. Typically, the alloy has two coats of copper plating which sandwiches nickel or something similar in between. The chromium plating goes on top. The process is expensive and complicated and not worth the effort considering the availability and price of new replacements from the many specialist Mini outlets. Fitting plastic chrome strips to the wheelarches is simple provided you immerse each strip in hot water to temporarily soften it.

Bring your Mini up to these specifications – both mechanically and visually – and you will have (dare I say it?) a car on a par with a Cooper, missing only its legendary name.

Mini facts and Mini-lore

Some things you may or may not have known:

- The Mini was the first British-built small car to feature an exhaust catalyst.

- The Mini has used more SU carburettors than any other car in SU's history.

- The last of the classic Minis may be considered outdated but they are on a par with today's offerings in featuring a driver's airbag, front seat belt tensioners, door beams and a 1.3-litre, fuel-injected engine with full closed-loop exhaust catalyst.

- In contrast with the Mini's economical image, the Rover Group commissioned a special Mini limousine for the Frankfurt motor show in 1997 featuring a satellite navigation system, a hand-built stereo system and air-conditioned seats. The cost was a cool £50,000.

- The Mini received an 'overdrive' fourth gear in 1997 which was the equivalent of a fifth gear on other cars. At 70mph engine speed was cut from 3888 to 3333rpm for more comfortable and quieter cruising.

- Sir Alec Issigonis, although undeniably a genius, failed his maths exams three times at Battersea Technical College, but fortunately was not put off pursuing a career in automotive engineering.

- The Mini undoubtedly accelerated the decline in the British motorcycle industry, whose products hitherto had provided the less well-to-do with their most affordable means of everyday transport. The Mini was also partly responsible for the decline in scooter sales, an ironic situation because at one stage the company also owned the Lambretta manufacturers, Innocenti.

- The Mini was the first car to feature a transverse engine driving the front wheels with a gearbox in the sump, a concept which has since been copied by virtually every competitor producing a supermini.

- The Mini's penchant for darting through traffic and running rings round larger cars gave rise to the popular sticker: 'You've just been Mini'd'.

- Although BMC's works drivers initially dreaded competing in Minis, regarding it almost as a punishment, after Rauno Aaltonen won the 1963 Alpine Rally with a 1071cc Mini Cooper they all wanted to abandon their Austin-Healeys.

- During the car's golden years of competition, 1965-67, the Mini scored 22 victories in international rallies, Aaltonen being the top scorer amongst the works team drivers with eight victories.

- A Mini was built with an engine at each end, boasting a total of 2.5 litres and 175bhp and capable of spinning all four wheels on take-off.

- At the last count there were more than 150 Mini clubs and registers in Great Britain alone, but internationally the Japanese trumped everybody with about 400 of them.

- The 12-inch wheel was standardized in 1984. It provided virtually the same rolling radius as the original 10-inch wheels thanks to lower-profile tyres.

- The Mini holds the distinction of being one of the few cars to have been listed in the dictionary as a generic description: 'Mini (mi-ni) 1964 – shortened form of minicar'. The term, of course, was derived from the word miniature and was also adopted by the fashion world, hence the miniskirt.

- The Mini is no stranger to stardom, the 1964 Monte Carlo Rally-winning car having been flown home to make a special appearance on the top television programme 'Sunday Night at the London Palladium', and of course in Cooper form a team of them played a major role in the Michael Caine film 'The Italian Job'.

- Niki Lauda first found motorsport success behind the wheel of a Mini Cooper in a hill-climb, and has since owned at least two road-going Minis.

- Famous Mini owners have included Enzo Ferrari (he had three), Brigitte Bardot, Peter Sellers, Spike Milligan, fashion guru Zandra Rhodes and Joanna Lumley.

- When launched the Mini was Spartan, the single-speed heater being an extra-cost option, there was no provision for a radio, and you had to pump the windscreen washers manually.

- Joanne Westlake was believed to be the first person to be born in a Mini, but not the last.

- If every Mini made was parked bumper-to-bumper, the line would stretch from London to Sydney, Australia, a distance of almost 10,600 miles.

- The first million Minis were produced by 1965, the second million by 1969 and the third million by 1972, and with a production run of more than 5.3 million it is the most successful British car ever.

- The record for a Mini 'cram' is 66 people, who took part on the Noel Edmonds 'Late Late Breakfast Show' in May 1986.

- Ringo Starr had his Mini converted into a hatchback in order to carry his drum kit around.

- The Mini's production run spanned well over a third of the entire history of the UK motor industry, which celebrated its centenary in 1996.